# THE AVOCADO COOKBOOK

OTHER BOOKS BY HELEN BAUER

*California Mission Days*

*California Rancho Days*

*California Gold Days*

*California Indian Days*

*Hawaii: The Aloha State*

*Water: Riches or Ruin*

*Japanese Festivals* (WITH SHERWIN CARLQUIST)

# The AVOCADO Cookbook

### HELEN BAUER
### *and*
### ROBERTA LOGERMAN

*Garden City, New York*
DOUBLEDAY & COMPANY, INC.

*To our families*

*Library of Congress Catalog Card Number 67-11152*
*Copyright © 1967 by Helen Bauer and Roberta Logerman*

"We may live without poetry, music and art;
We may live without conscience and live without heart;
We may live without friends; we may live without books;
But civilized man cannot live without cooks."

OWEN MEREDITH
(*Edward Robert Bulwer, Earl of Lytton*)

# Contents

# List of Illustrations

## BLACK AND WHITE

## COLOR

# List of Recipes by Category

[*Consult Index for page numbers*]

## APPETIZERS

### HORS D'OEUVRES, PICK-UPS, NIBBLERS

Avocado Fritters I
Avocado Fritters II
Avocado Stuffed Celery
Cocktail Tidbit
Cream Puff Nibblers

Green Velvet Appetizers
Smoked Beef Hors d'Oeuvres
Tomato-Avocado Hors
   d'Oeuvres
"Quickie" Ideas

### CANAPÉS

Avocado Spread, Basic
Bacon-Avocado Canapés
Dade County Canapés

Palm Springs Pâté Canapés
"Quickie" Idea

### DIPS AND DUNKS

Avocado Bacon Dip
Avocado Cottage Dip
Avocado Crunchy Dip
Avocado Seafood Dip
Avocado Tuna Dip
Avocumber Dip
Capri Shrimp Dip
Chili Avocado Dip

Crab Avocado Dip
Curried Avocado Dip
Dipsy Doodle Dip
Guacamole
Party Avocado Dip
Pip of a Dip
Shrimp Dip
"Quickie" Ideas

### COCKTAILS

*Fruit Cocktails*
Autumn Cocktail
Avocado Cranberry Frost
   Cocktail

Avocado Fruit Cocktail
Avocado Sunset Cocktail
California Sunshine Cup

## SANDWICHES, BREAD, AND MUFFINS

## COLD SANDWICHES

Avocado Bacon Sandwich
Spread
Avocado Dagwoods
Avocado Jelly Roll
Sandwiches
Avocado Seven Seas
Sandwiches
Avocado Swiss Sandwiches
Avocado Toppers
Avocado Tuna-Burgers
Avocado Turkey Club
Sandwiches
Big Boy Sandwiches
Captain's Special Sandwiches
Club Sandwiches de Luxe
Coronado Sandwiches

Crab Salad Club Sandwiches
Danish Sandwich Special
Deviled Avocado Sandwiches
Dutch Treat Sandwiches
Favorite Avocado Sandwich
Spread
Golden Gate Club Sandwich
Hamburger Delight Topper
Laguna Sandwich Filling
Norway Sandwich Spread
Pacific Paradise Sandwiches
Rancho Egg Sandwiches
Savory Avocado Sandwich
Filling
Seafood Sandwiches
Teen-Age Special Sandwiches

## BREAD

California Avocado Bread

## MUFFINS

Avocado Muffins
"Quickie" Ideas

## DESSERTS AND DESSERT SAUCES

### FROZEN DESSERTS

Avocado Cranberry Mousse
Avocado Bombe
Avocado Cream Freeze
Avocado Honey Ice Cream
Avocado Ice Cream, Polynesia
Avocado Marlow
Avocado Orange Ice
Avocado Raspberry Majestic
Avocado Sherbet Imperiale
Cathay Delight

Dreamwood Ice Cream
Favorite Frozen Pudding
Frozen Melba Pudding
Marmalade Mousse
Princess Frozen Dessert
Ramona Mousse
Sea-Foam Mousse
Summer Mousse Belvedere
Tropicana Ice Cream

# Preface and Acknowledgments

Preparing delicacies that will delight the most discriminating gourmet is the dream of almost every woman—or man—who enjoys being a "food artist." Intriguing specialty foods do not just happen; creativity and a certain amount of experimentation must go into their preparation. "The one who makes the experiment deservedly claims the honor and the reward," so said Horace (65–8 B.C.). Are you the venturesome type when it comes to trying out new flavors and combinations? Whether you are or not, why not be a "tryer-out"; take an adventure into Avocado Land.

This book of unusually good things to eat is a collection of recipes for foods possessing qualities of subtlety of combination and blend; affinity and contrast of flavors which bring surprises to the gourmet and fame to the hostess who prepares them. Try these recipes, as many as you can, and you will discover more ways of using avocados than you ever knew existed—and all of them brimming with goodness. Try topping hamburgers or a hot baked potato with an avocado mixture or use it instead of butter on a piping hot ear of corn. Make a special sauce for fish, meats, or seafood. The use of avocado in salads is legion. It becomes a filling for tortillas, sandwiches, hard-cooked eggs, tomatoes, or green peppers. See what it will do when added to soups at the last minute! No one can overlook the ubiquitous avocado dip, guacamole, so easily made or bought fresh-frozen ready to use. Who ever heard of avocado desserts, pies, cakes, bread, muffins, beverages? We have—and we are passing along these rare recipes to you. Go ahead—be venturesome—try preparing them all!

The simplest way of eating avocado is *au naturel* with just a dash of salt and a splash of fresh lime or lemon juice. This is the way the Mexican avocado eater says the avocado "tastes itself." In a certain sense this expresses the idea in avocado menu usage— to preserve the unequaled, subtle flavor of the avocado and to enhance the flavors of other foods with which it is combined. You can dice, cube, slice, mash, sieve or serve as a half-shell and still be assured that the accommodating fruit will blend with almost any ingredient used with it. It fits obligingly into *any* part of the menu and can be used for practically every occasion whether it be for breakfasts, brunches, luncheons, dinners, cocktail parties, buffets, or barbecues.

Have you ever heard ladies at a luncheon or elsewhere say, "Avocados are so wonderful—if they were not *so* terribly fattening! They have a million calories, you know!" For a ready refutation of this mistaken idea, read "The Avocado Story, Are You Counting Calories?"

Before starting (or continuing) on your road to fame as a "food artist" and a cook par excellence, read the story of this remarkable fruit that has been used as a staple food for centuries. As you proceed through succeeding pages of recipes, adventure from one category to another. Check the "Quickie" ideas at the end of each chapter to discover what impressive foods can be prepared in a matter of minutes. Throughout the book you will find many unusual and inexpensive ways of using avocados for family fare as well as surprising food ideas for happy entertaining. We predict that before long you too will become an avocado fancier. It's the fashionable thing to be!

Since the authors, mother and daughter, both enjoy cooking (and eating), the compilation of recipes for this book was a happy assignment. Avocados for testing recipes were easily available from Bauer's Bendita Rancho (Santa Barbara) and our respective families were the recipients of our culinary efforts. Family members repaid with their patience and understanding during the time-consuming period of manuscript preparation. To Roy M. Bauer, avocado grower and daily helper and to Calvin G. Logerman, for interest and encouragement and to Lynn Ann and Gail Ellen Logerman, who helped in their own special ways, we offer our affectionate appreciation.

It is impossible to overestimate the credit due and hereby given in full measure to the Calavo Growers of California. The organization furnished all the pictorial material in this book, both color plates and black and white photographs. We were the fortunate recipients of their hundreds of recipes which were collected through years of food research. The organization staff members gave unstintingly of their time and background of experience in reading the manuscript for authenticity of content. Those who were particularly helpful and to whom we offer our unreserved sense of obligation and gratitude include: Mr. T. E. Lynn Preston, advertising sales promotion manager; Mrs. Kay Berger, home economist; Mr. J. C. Shepherd, publicity and public relations. A special word of appreciation is due Mr. Robert P. Rich, Calavo field representative, who gave cheerfully and generously of his time and information. Thanks are hereby given to Mr. George E. Roesch, Fallbrook (California) Avocado Festival director (1966) for his active interest in this project.

Appreciation and credit is given herewith to the members of the editorial staff of the publisher for capable assistance and friendly understanding.

# Introduction—
# The Avocado Story

## THOSE WISE AZTECS

Is the exotic subtropical avocado with its smooth, nutlike flavor a new fruit? It may come as a surprise to those who know little or nothing about the avocado that the increasingly popular fruit was eaten and enjoyed by the Mayans of Mexico three hundred years before Christ was born. The ancient Aztecs of Mexico, who had long used the fruit as a staple food, drew hieroglyphics to symbolize the "place where the avocado abounds."

Their name for the fruit was *ahuacatl* or *aocatl*, later corrupted by Spanish to *ahuacate* or *aguacate*. The Mayans of Yucatán and Guatemala knew it as the *okh* or *on* and the Peruvians called it *palta;* the Colombians, the *cura.* The Zapotecs of southern Mexico called it (and still do), the *yasu* and *isu,* while the Tarascans (western Mexico) know it as the *cupanda.* In Honduras and El Salvador it was known as *narimu,* and in Nicaragua and Costa Rica the names of *amo* and *devora* were used.

Many foods have fascinating historical backgrounds, but few have as romantic and long a history as the avocado. Early explorers extolled the virtues of the fruit they found under cultivation from northern South America to Mexico. A Spaniard, Martín Fernández de Enciso, a man of learning who was a cartographer, was responsible for an announcement to the Old World of a fruit "which is marvelous of flavor, so good and pleasing to the palate that it is a marvelous thing." This was in the year 1519, after he had found the amazing fruit on an expedition he accompanied to the northern coast of South America.

Next, Gonzalo Fernando de Oviedo, who had spent much time at the Spanish court, came to America and after travel and observation made a report to Charles V about the wonders of the New World. Among the wonders, he gave an account of a fruit which he described as being something like a pear yet not a pear but one of very good eating and taste.

In succeeding years, other adventurers reported seeing the fruit in several countries. Francisco Cervantes Salazar, an adventurer from South America to Mexico, recorded in 1554 that he found the fruit in a public market in Tenochtitlán, present-day Mexico City. An English merchant named Hawkes wrote an account in 1589 which may have been the first one in the English language, in which he spoke of the fruit *alvacata*. In 1672, an English physician to the king, W. Hughes, traveled to Jamaica and there tasted the fruit. In his enthusiasm he wrote, "it nourisheth and strengtheneth the body exceedingly." He described the fruit as being as soft and tender as the pulp of a pippin and thought it to be the most rare and pleasant fruit of that island. It is known that George Washington visited Barbados in 1751; ate the *avogato* pears, and pronounced them the most admired fruit grown there.

During the long period of its evolution, over forty picturesque names were given to the fruit such as: butter pear, custard apple, laurel peach, and vegetable marrow. As time went on and familiarity with the avocado became more general, there was a divergence of opinion as to the correct name of this fruit. Finally, in Florida, where the avocado made its entrance from the West Indies, the misleading appellation of "alligator pear" was given to it. One conjectured reason for the name was that it had a rough skin like an alligator and was the shape of a pear. Today, this outmoded name should be relegated to limbo and forgotten. California had avocado plantings also but the growers there clung tenaciously to the Mexican name, *aguacate*. At the beginning of the twentieth century, the American Pomological Society and the United States Department of Agriculture officially approved the name avocado, probably the English version derived from the various Spanish names.

No matter what the name given to the fruit through the centuries or in whatever country it was found, there was universal agreement about one basic fact—the fruit was unlike any other, one that was "fit for the gods," to be enjoyed and respected. Yes, those Aztecs of long ago and those who followed after them were wise indeed in discovering the delectable fruit—as are a growing number of American families today.

## AN INDUSTRY IS BORN

Enthusiastic explorers helped to popularize the avocado in places where the avocado was unknown. Wherever it was introduced, it shortly became a staple item in the diet. Attempts were made to grow avocados in Europe as early as 1600, but the climate was too cold. The first known attempt to grow them in the United States with any degree of success was near Miami, Florida, in the year 1833. It is possible, but not proven, that the Franciscan padres cherished avocado seeds that grew into seedlings in California's mission gardens (1769–1823). The first confirmed California avocado planting was in 1858, but it was not until after the turn of the century that there was serious interest in avocado production.

Early-day growers enlisted the aid of plant explorers to seek out superior strains and varieties, mostly in areas of South America. Wilson Popenoe, associated with the United States Department of Agriculture, spent nine years and traveled thousands of miles to secure budwood specimens from chosen varieties for experimental planting. It was found that imported varieties throve well in the mild climates of California and Florida. It was not long before there was a demand for nursery trees budded to the best available seedlings. Nurserymen in California used Mexican-type rootstock because the seed was relatively plentiful, inexpensive, and more resistant to cold than the Guatemalan variety.

In 1915, pioneers in the industry formed the California Avocado Association (now Society), the primary purpose being to improve production of the avocado, classify varieties, and engage in a research program—a purpose from which the society has not deviated to this day. From that time on, avocados became a genuine business venture, and a new industry was born, albeit a small one during the early years of commercial enterprise.

## AN INDUSTRY GROWS

As consumer demand for avocados was fostered, so grew the industry. It was early determined that, since a major industry appeared to be in the making, there should be a marketing organization that would enable growers to do together what they could not do as individual growers. By pooling production and distribution, growers would be able to fill market needs with the desired kind of merchandise at the right time and place.

In 1923, the California Avocado Association led the way and a sponsored grower-controlled and -owned co-operative marketing organization came into being—the California Avocado Growers Exchange, later renamed Calavo Growers of California. The name CALAVO came about as a result of a contest. With the aid of the press, the newly formed co-operative launched a nation-wide search for a name that would identify quality products to the consumer. Thousands of names were suggested, and the one chosen was CALAVO, a combination of the first three letters of CALifornia and AVOcado, a name registered by the United States Patent Office.

The primary purpose of the growers' association has been to promote the interests of its members in the development and advancement of California's avocado industry and provide the consumer with the finest quality fruit at a fair price. In order to do this there must be an orderly, consistent flow of avocados to market throughout the seasons, a careful handling of fruit from trees to markets, and the selection of fruit picked at maturity and tested for superior quality and flavor. There must be a skillful geographical distribution based on specific markets, and Calavo is the only marketer in the avocado industry with its own representation in major markets throughout the country. This association has, through years of laboratory testing and marketing experience, developed a standard higher than that set up by the California Agricultural Code for avocados. Only fruit of a limited number of varieties that meet rigid requirements for oil content (not less than 8 per cent but usually more), flavor, shape, color, appearance, ripening and keeping qualities, receive the famous golden CALAVO stamp. It is a hallmark of quality and the consumer can be assured that any avocado bearing this stamp is of top grade at the time of packing.

There are a number of independently owned avocado marketing companies in California, commission houses, and one smaller co-operative, but Calavo Growers of California (with 60 per cent of the industry's trees in the state) remains the largest marketer. In 1966, Calavo acquired the majority interest in the Lucerne Packing Company, Dade County, Florida, to increase its position in the marketing of a substantial percentage of Florida's avocado crop. Tonnage from California and Florida groves furnishes millions of pounds of the fruit to the consumer. No longer just a venture, the avocado industry has assumed a position of being one of the important specialty industries in these states, essentially the source of all United States avocado production.

## WHAT WILL THEY DO WITH THE AVOCADO NEXT?

Present indications are that the industry will continue to grow. A course has been charted for the future that is bold, aggressive, and exciting to contemplate. One reason for this is to meet the needs of the consumer who is discovering the almost limitless ways of using this congenial fruit that blends with such a variety of other foods. The California Avocado Advisory Board, an industry-supported organization, seeks to acquaint modern homemakers with the flavorful, nutritious fruit that can be prepared so easily, inexpensively, and in such a variety of ways.

Even though millions of pounds of avocados have been purchased from stores and markets through the past years, not all of the fruit will go to the nation's fruit stands and supermarkets coast to coast. Beginning in 1964, Calavo perfected a new and exclusive fast-freezing process (cryogenic) using liquid nitrogen at minus 320 degrees Fahrenheit. It uses space-age techniques and temperatures that are colder than the dark side of the moon. Unlike earlier attempts to freeze avocados, the new process avoids breakdown of fruit structure or deterioration of taste. Once frozen, the new Calavo products may be held for a year or more at normal freezer temperatures and thawed in minutes for immediate use. The fruit is conditioned before freezing. Experts determine the proper ripeness at the time of freezing and the fruit is fast-frozen at this point. This means that ready-to-eat avocado half-shells, slices, cubes, and the like may be purchased in the frozen food section of the supermarket. The first such frozen product introduced to the general public was the flavorsome dip guacamole (7¾-ounce and 16-ounce cans). It's a great idea—a wonderful ready-to-eat product to have in the freezer for unexpected or planned occasions, to be used as a dip or in other ways. With this new "flash-freezing" method, refrigerated fresh avocados can be shipped all over the world. So the door is open even wider for broader use of the avocado through "cold magic."*

## PLACES WHERE THE AVOCADO ABOUNDS

The avocado (Persea) is subtropical and therefore restricted to suitable climates. It is a member of the laurel family, with such relatives as sassafras, cinnamon, camphor, and California bay. Climates that are suitable for growing avocados include parts of Mexico, Central and South America, the West Indies, Australia, New Zealand, South Africa, Egypt, Israel, and certain Pacific islands, including Hawaii. In the United States, California is by far the leader in commercial avocado production, with about twenty-five thousand acres in areas from Santa Barbara to San Diego, with more than half the productive acreage in San Diego County. Florida's commercial avocado groves are located close to Miami in Dade County, with about seven thousand acres planted with avocados.

It takes about five years before a young avocado tree will bear fruit commercially. The annual crop is not consistent and the grower is never certain of the yield. The avocado may thrive one year and under similar conditions produce less the next year. Some varieties bear more consistently than others (Hass, for example). When an annual crop is plentiful, prices for the fruit are less; when in short supply, prices are higher. Even when the consumer has to pay slightly more than usual at times, the price per avocado is still very reasonable. It is no longer considered a luxury food, and the versatility of use and high nutritional value make it one of the best values to be found in the food market today.

* At President Lyndon Johnson's inauguration dinner, five thousand people were served fresh-frozen avocados.

## VARIETIES OF AVOCADOS

The appearance of the avocado skin, which varies according to variety, should not puzzle the buyer. Who eats the skin? Whatever the color or kind of skin, the consumer can be assured of almost uniform smooth, fine-flavored fruit.

Even the experienced avocado user will be surprised to know that many more than five hundred varieties of avocado have been catalogued. Only about a hundred have been grown commercially with relatively few of that number grown in any quantity. Varieties are classified into two main types (three races): the Mexican-Guatemalan (and hybrids) type, grown in California, and the West Indian (and hybrids), grown in Florida. Varieties differ in color and kind of skin, size and shape of fruit, and in size of seed.

To meet consumer demands, avocados are harvested the year around in the United States, depending upon maturity of varieties. The well-known Fuerte (which constitutes about 60 per cent of the total crop), a smooth, green-skinned fruit introduced from Mexico, is considered a winter variety usually marketed from November to May. The word *fuerte* means strong, so-named because the variety survived a very cold winter years ago. Second in volume (and presently growing in tonnage) is the Hass, a very popular dark-skinned summer variety marketed from May through November. The Hass was named after a postal employee who patented the variety. The Florida season embraces late summer, fall, and early winter.

Fortunately, a continuous study of avocado varieties has been carried on for many years by a committee sponsored by the California Avocado Society and comprised of experienced avocado growers and research horticulturists specializing in avocado culture. Such research helps growers to know what varieties bear fruit consistently, market well, and have the highest quality fruit.

At present there are thick-skin and thin-skin varieties—green, black, and purplish ones; smooth skins and pebbly skins; round and pear-shaped fruit with long necks and short necks. Some have been known to weigh several pounds; others get no bigger than three ounces. Whatever the color of the skin or the shape of the fruit, under the skin lies a golden heart of goodness!

## AND SO TO MARKET

When avocados are mature (oil content constitutes one of the main criteria in determining maturity), they are ready to be picked. To avoid skin bruise, each avocado is clipped from the tree and the stem cut flush to the fruit; this to prevent long stems from injuring the fruit. Avocados are then placed in the harvester's canvas picking bag. Either a ladder or a pole-picker, that has clippers and a small canvas bag on the end is needed to pick fruit from the uppermost branches. Pickers put fruit from their picking bags into field boxes and trucks deliver the boxes to refrigerated rooms in the nearest packing house. Each fruit lot is numbered so as to indicate the source, quantity, and variety.

In the packing house of the growers' association, the fruit is put on a long, moving conveyor belt, and before it reaches the end of the line, it has been dusted, polished, graded, weighed, and stamped with the appropriate brand name to designate its quality. Then it is ready to be carefully packed, put aboard refrigerated trucks or freight cars—thence to markets from coast to coast and border to border. No more than thirty days normally elapses from picking to eating, and at every stage between the avocado is given the utmost in care.

## ARE YOU COUNTING CALORIES?

So you think avocados are fattening? The unique avocado is creamy in texture, is nutlike in flavor, and contains fruit oil, and because of these virtues people have been led to believe that avocados are high in caloric content and therefore fattening. A basic fact often overlooked is that it is not *what* people eat that makes them fat; it's *how much!* A person can gain weight by eating too much meat!

The avocado, like milk, is almost a perfect food and its digestibility nearly approaches that of whole milk. Some pediatricians, for instance, recommend it as the first solid food in the baby's diet. Hospitals have found that the emulsified oil found in avocados is especially acceptable to patients requiring easily digested foods.

The most common serving of avocado is the half-shell (about 5 ounces), which for the calorie counter means less than 150 calories—well under the count of many everyday foods. The average serving in an unmolded salad is less than 75 calories. Many dieters enjoy an avocado half-shell for luncheon with only fresh lime or lemon juice to season it. It is their claim that it satisfies the appetite at a very low cost of calories. Compare the calorie count of other foods:

|  | Amount | Calories |
|---|---|---|
| Frankfurter | 1 | 155 |
| Plain gelatin dessert | 1 cup | 140 |
| Milk (whole) | 1 cup | 160 |
| Fruit cocktail, canned | 1 cup | 195 |
| Eggs | 2 | 160 |
| Hamburger patty | ¼ pound | 245 |
| Baked custard | 1 cup | 285 |

—*From United States Department of Agriculture, 1959*

No other fruit contains such a wealth of nutritive values. Besides other factors mentioned, there is a bonus of eleven health-giving vitamins among which are: A (carotene), $B_1$ (thiamine), $B_2$ (riboflavin), C (ascorbic acid), E, K, pantothenic acid, HH (biotin) and folic acid. In addition, there are fourteen basic minerals present, the most important of which are iron, copper, calcium, potassium, manganese, sodium, and phosphorus, and in the proportion that Nature intended them to be in order to be properly utilized by the body. The avocado is one of the rare fruits having no starch and very little sugar. The average protein content of an avocado is 2.1 per cent, an unusual amount for fruits.

All of these favorable qualities mean that the avocado, with its minerals, vitamins, and easily digested fruit oil, goes a long way in supplying minimum daily food requirements. What other food has so much to offer with so few well-spent calories?

## THE WISE SHOPPER

Did you ever hear of anyone who picked and ate an avocado from the tree? Never! Even though the fruit is in the process of developing for six months to a year or more before maturation and by marketing requirements is "ripe," the fruit is not usable as long as it remains firm.

Unlike many other fresh fruits, the buyer cannot tell the real eating quality by looking at or feeling an avocado. She can test for ripeness, however. At the market, don't pinch the avocados! Pinching is apt to bruise them and cause dark spots to appear. To test for ripeness, cup the avocado in the palm of the hand. If it "gives" or feels soft to gentle pressure, it is ready to be used. Thick-skinned varieties require a little more pressure. An easy way to test them for ripeness is to insert a toothpick into the stem end; if it goes in easily, the fruit is eating-ripe.*

Unless an avocado is needed for immediate use, it is preferable to buy firm fruit and let it ripen at normal room temperature, which usually takes only a few days. The wise shopper often buys several avocados at one time. While ripening, some can be used as part of a table arrangement. Some can be stored in the refrigerator (never the freezer) to delay the ripening process although they should not be kept there long. The best way is to let the fruit ripen at room temperature and then put it in the refrigerator, where it will keep well for several days.†

## THE CLEVER COOK

There are numerous and attractive ways that the clever cook can utilize avocados. Follow these simple directions:

*Avocado Half-Shells (Unpeeled)*
   (1) Cut avocado into halves lengthwise, but do not peel.
   (2) Twist halves slightly to separate halves; don't try to pull them apart.
   (3) Strike seed with sharp edge of a knife, twist, and lift seed out.

   * Fresh-frozen avocado products are eating-ripe; only thawing for a few minutes is necessary.
   † If part of avocado is unused, leave seed in, brush with lemon juice, cover with transparent wrap, and refrigerate.

*Avocado Balls*
Cut fruit out of unpeeled half-shell with melon-ball cutter or rounded half-teaspoon measuring spoon.

*Avocado Half-Shells (Peeled)*
Halve and seed avocado. To remove skin put half-shell down in palm of hand and strip or pull off skin beginning at the narrow or stem end. The dark-skinned variety will not peel quite so easily, but usually no actual paring is necessary.

*Lengthwise Slices*
Lay halves flat side down and cut lengthwise slices of desired width.

*Crescents or Half-Moons*
Cut lengthwise slices in half to form crescents or half-moons. These can be used as decorative pinwheels or in fan shapes, overlapping or two together to form a round salad base.

*Cubed or Diced\**
Cut lengthwise slices, then cube each slice. Dice in the same way except cut into smaller pieces.

*Mashed or Sieved†*
Well-softened avocados may be mashed easily by using a fork and crushing pulp against the side of the bowl. If finer texture is desired, fruit can be sieved through a coarse strainer. While a blender is fast and efficient, its use is not absolutely essential.

*Rings*
Cut unpeeled avocado in half crosswise; twist to remove seed. cut slices crosswise of desired width, then peel each individual ring.

\* 1 small avocado=about 12 bite-sized cubes
1 medium-sized avocado=about 24 bite-sized cubes
1 large avocado=about 36 bite-sized cubes
† 1 small avocado, sieved=⅓ to ½ cup
1 medium-sized avocado, sieved=about ⅔ cup
1 large avocado, sieved=1⅓ to 1½ cups

If you buy frozen fresh avocados, follow a few simple rules for thawing. They may be prepared while partially frozen if you allow time for the thawing process to continue before serving. Treatment of the frozen avocado, once thawed, is the same as the fresh fruit. Time for thawing varies according to the temperature of the place of thawing (room temperature is usually considered to be 72°). Here are a few instructions to remember:

*Avocado Half-Shell (Unpeeled)*
Remove from package and place on nonmetallic surface, cavity side down, and thaw at room temperature from 1 to 1¼ hours.

*Avocado Half-Shell (Peeled)*
Remove from package. Rotate each frozen half, skin side up, under warm tap water for about 20 seconds. Remove the skin. Place half-shell cavity side down on nonmetallic surface. Squeeze lemon or lime juice over the exposed fruit. Leave at room temperature to thaw about 1 hour. The halves can be cut into slices after thawing.

*Avocado Slices*
Slices thaw rapidly and you can use them in assembling most dishes. If desired, spread the frozen slices in a single layer on a nonmetallic surface and leave at room temperature from 20 to 25 minutes. Once thawed, wrap and keep in refrigerator until ready to serve.

This is not the end of the Avocado Story. It should be just the beginning. The rest is up to you. With a new understanding of and appreciation for the exotic avocado and with the scores of recipes of all kinds at your command, you are ready to start on an exciting and rewarding adventure of gastronomical discovery into Avocado Land. Let it be said of your home, "This is the place where the avocado abounds!"

# *Appetizers*

"Epicurean cooks
Sharpen with cloyless sauce his appetite."
—William Shakespeare, *Antony and Cleopatra*

Appetizers that serve as an introduction to dinner or are served as cocktail fare include a variety of hors d'oeuvres, canapés, dips, and cocktails. Hors d'oeuvres consist of pickup foods such as tidbits, snacks, and nibblers. Canapés, either hot or cold, are served in endless designs having inviting spreads and decorations. The popular dip that has won international fame is the avocado dip guacamole. All kinds of appetizers may be passed to guests or served from the buffet table.

There is a current custom of serving cocktails, such as fruit, seafood, and vegetable, as a first course at dinner in lieu of the salad course. Whatever appetizers are served or in whatever manner, it should be remembered that they should dazzle the eye and tease the appetite—nothing more.

## HORS D'OEUVRES, PICKUPS, NIBBLERS

Hors d'oeuvres should be appetite "teasers" and therefore never large nor very rich. Attractive hor d'oeuvres will provide a good start for the social event and give partakers a sense of confidence in the dinner courses to follow.

## AVOCADO FRITTERS I

There are several interesting ways to prepare these unusual mouth-watering, sizzling hors d'oeuvres. They may be served bite-sized or, if larger avocado cubes are used, as a main dish on a meatless day or as an accompaniment for a meat or fish course. If an appetizer, be careful not to let the delighted guests eat too many; remind them that dinner is ahead.

|  | or | QUICK METHOD: |
|---|---|---|
| *1 cup flour* | | *1 cup prepared biscuit mix* |
| *½ teaspoon salt* | | *1 egg, beaten* |
| *2 teaspoons baking powder* | | *⅔ cup milk* |
| *1 egg, beaten* | | *1 teaspoon Worcestershire* |
| *½ cup milk* | | *sauce* |
| *1 teaspoon Worcestershire* | | *1 large avocado* |
| *sauce* | | |
| *1 large avocado* | | |

Mix dry ingredients (or use prepared biscuit mix). Add beaten egg to milk and Worcestershire sauce; stir into dry ingredients. Cut avocado into cubes or crescent shapes. Dip cubes into batter and deep-fry in oil at 375° for 2 to 4 minutes until golden brown. Serve piping hot either plain or with a catsup-lemon juice dip.

Makes as many servings as there are avocado pieces.

## AVOCADO FRITTERS II

| | |
|---|---|
| *1 large avocado* | *4 teaspoons baking powder* |
| *Garlic salt* | *Evaporated milk diluted with* |
| *2 eggs, beaten* | *water (use enough liquid* |
| *Dash Worcestershire sauce* | *to make batter that will* |
| *1 teaspoon salt* | *stick to the avocado* |
| *⅔ cup refined cornstarch* | *pieces)* |
| *½ teaspoon pepper* | |

Cut avocado into desired shapes; sprinkle with garlic salt. Beat eggs, add Worcestershire sauce; add dry ingredients. Gradually add milk-water mixture to make a smooth batter. Dip avocado pieces into batter; fry in oil 375° for 2 to 4 minutes until golden brown. Serve very hot.

Makes as many servings as avocado pieces and according to appreciative appetites. If a crowd, better make plenty.

## AVOCADO STUFFED CELERY

Crisp, crunchy celery sticks with avocado filling make for an ideal predinner appetizer.

1 medium-sized avocado
2 tablespoons fresh lemon
   juice
1 teaspoon salt
1 teaspoon grated onion
Dash cayenne

2 tablespoons sweet pickle
   relish
2 tablespoons chopped
   pimiento
Celery

Mash or sieve avocado. Blend in lemon juice, salt, onion, cayenne, pickle relish, and pimiento. Heap into 2-inch stalks of celery. Makes about ¾ cup of filling. Another method is to separate and wash celery sticks; put them together again with the filling; tie up and chill. Before serving, cut in thin slices crosswise.

Makes as many servings as sticks or slices of celery.

## COCKTAIL TIDBIT

An unusual cocktail tidbit that can be made in a hurry.

1 medium-sized avocado
Mayonnaise
Fresh lemon or lime juice

1 small package potato chips,
   crushed

Cut peeled avocado into bite-sized pieces; dip in mayonnaise that has been thinned with lemon or lime juice and roll in crushed potato chips. Serve on cocktail picks.

Makes about 24 cubes.

## CREAM PUFF NIBBLERS

Here's an entirely new way to serve little cream puffs.

½ package (1 stick) cream
  puff mix
1 medium-sized avocado
1 3-ounce package cream
  cheese
1 teaspoon salt

1 teaspoon chicken stock
½ teaspoon onion juice
½ cup whipping cream
Jumbo ripe olives
Curry-toasted walnut halves

Make bite-sized cream puffs by using package directions for miniature cream puffs. Cool. Mash avocado; work in with cream cheese. Stir in seasonings. Whip cream into soft mounds, not too stiff. Fold into avocado mixture and salt to taste. Add a little green food coloring if desired. Just before serving, cut tops from cream puffs; fill with avocado cream mixture. Arrange on tray; garnish with olives and walnut halves that have been toasted until crisp in curry-flavored butter.

Makes about 40 bite-sized cream puffs.

## GREEN VELVET APPETIZERS

You will find this an impressive and surprising appetizer.

1 medium-sized avocado
½ pound butter or
  margarine (at room
  temperature)
½ envelope plain gelatin

2 tablespoons table cream
2 tablespoons boiling water
2 tablespoons lemon juice
Garlic or onion salt
  (optional)

Mash or sieve avocado; add soft butter or margarine and blend well. Soften gelatin in cream; dissolve in boiling water. Add gelatin to avocado mixture, along with lemon juice and garlic salt if used. Turn into shallow square pan and spread out smoothly to about ½-inch depth. Cover and chill thoroughly. Cut into small squares or individual servings. Serve with toothpicks.

Makes about 32 appetizers.

## SMOKED BEEF HORS D'OEUVRES

This is a new taste sensation. Try it!

1 medium-sized avocado
Fresh lemon or lime juice
Salt

Thinly sliced smoked dried beef

Cut avocado into ½-inch cubes; dip in lemon or lime juice and sprinkle lightly with salt. Wrap each cube with a slice of dried beef; fasten with a cocktail pick.

Makes about 24 appetizers.

## TOMATO-AVOCADO HORS D'OEUVRES

Guests will find this a perfect pickup and so attractive on the tray.

Cherry tomatoes
1 medium-sized avocado
Lemon juice

Lettuce
Green pepper case
Thousand Island dressing

Peel tiny cherry tomatoes and spear each with a pick. Cut balls from avocado by using a regular ball cutter or a ¼-teaspoon round measuring spoon. Dip balls into lemon juice and spear each with a pick. Arrange cherry tomatoes and avocado balls on plate with lettuce. In center, put the pepper case or a fancy bowl filled with Thousand Island dressing. Tomatoes and avocado balls can then be dipped into dressing before eating.

Makes about 20 avocado balls, depending on size.

## "QUICKIE" IDEAS

Fascinating appetizer kabobs can be made by alternating avocado and Vienna sausage cubes and ripe olives on a pick. Use your imagination with all sorts of such interesting combinations.

A zippy mayonnaise spread on crackers just before serving and topped with thin slices of avocado and pimiento strips makes excellent party-time nibblers.

## CANAPÉS

Canapés, which are quite different from sandwiches, are thin slices of bread, either toasted or left plain. The bread should be cut in fancy shapes: diamonds, triangles, rectangles, circles, squares, crescents. Decorations or garnishes are limited only by the artistry of the canapé maker. Nothing is quite so tempting to the eye or palate as an ample supply of canapés shaped and decorated in infinite variety. Canapés can be made ahead; stored in the freezer, and before serving time thawed in the refrigerator to maintain freshness. If canapés taste as good as they look, the display will disappear in minutes.

## AVOCADO SPREAD, BASIC

A basic avocado spread may be used for canapés, sandwiches, or as a topping for hot baked potatoes.

| | |
|---|---|
| *1 large avocado, sieved* | *¼ teaspoon garlic salt* |
| *¼ teaspoon salt* | *1½ teaspoons lemon juice* |

Combine all ingredients and blend thoroughly. Use on any canapé, cracker, Melba toast, as a sandwich spread, stuffing for celery, or on a baked potato.

VARIATIONS:

To the basic spread add finely chopped ripe or green olives, chopped hard-cooked eggs, pickle relish, minced pimiento, chopped green pepper, or any seafood. Decorate with paprika, sieved egg yolk, or white, curled anchovies, radish rounds, thinly sliced cucumber, sliced stuffed olives, thin pickle rounds, or minced parsley.

## BACON-AVOCADO CANAPÉS

For an intriguing flavor combination, you will like this.

Roll up a slice of bacon for each person and fasten roll with a toothpick. Put rolls on cake rack on a baking sheet or shallow baking pan and heat in 350° oven until bacon rolls are crisp, about 15 to 20 minutes. Toast canapé rounds of bread on one side only; butter the other side. Cut thin crosswise slices of peeled avocado. Place an avocado ring on each toast round; put bacon roll in center of each avocado ring after removing toothpick.

Makes a variable number, depending on amount of ingredients used.

## DADE COUNTY CANAPÉS

These canapés are as easy to do as 1-2-3 and so tasty!

Mash a ripe medium-sized avocado and season with lemon juice and onion salt to taste. Spread on canapé bases, toasted on one side. Top with thin strip of bacon; put under the broiler and broil until bacon is crisp. Variations include pimientos, grated cheese, or finely chopped almonds.

Makes about ¾ cup of spread.

## PALM SPRINGS PÂTÉ CANAPÉS

Here's something new that you may wish to serve many times.

| | |
|---|---|
| 1 tablespoon butter or margarine | Dash pepper |
| 2 teaspoons chicken stock | 1 pound chicken livers |
| ¼ cup minced onion | 2 tablespoons sherry |
| ½ cup water | 2 medium-sized avocados |
| ½ teaspoon salt | Lemon juice |
| | Crisp crackers |

Melt butter or margarine in saucepan. Add stock, onion, water, seasonings, chicken livers, and sherry. Bring to boil; reduce heat and simmer covered about 20 minutes or until chicken livers are tender. Place mixture in blender and whir until smooth, or strain, saving liquid and put livers through fine food grinder. Mix with reserved liquid. Pour into dish with cover and chill several hours or overnight. Just before serving, halve, peel and seed avocados; cut into about 30 thin slices. Sprinkle with lemon juice. Spread crisp crackers or toasted canapé rounds generously with *pâté* and avocado slices.
Makes 30 canapés.


## "QUICKIE" IDEA

Avocado anchovy snack spread: One of the easiest canapé spreads is to blend together ½ cup mashed avocado with ¼ cup sour cream and 4 teaspoons anchovy paste. Spread on canapé bases or crackers, or it can be used as a dip.


## DIPS AND DUNKS

Savory dips help to get an occasion off to a good start, especially if avocado is one of the important ingredients. The clever hostess has either dips made ahead or the makings for them in the refrigerator or freezer. In addition, she has a supply of potato chips, corn chips, Melba toast, or fancy crackers for dunking into dips. An unusual receptacle for dips is the avocado half-shell.

## AVOCADO BACON DIP

Tempt guests with the taste treat of this dip.

2 medium-sized avocados
½ teaspoon onion salt
1 tablespoon lemon or lime juice

4 crisp-cooked bacon slices, crumbled
Few drops Tabasco sauce
1 hard-cooked egg, sieved

Mash or sieve avocados; combine with rest of ingredients except egg and blend well. Refrigerate in covered dish for at least an hour. To serve, sprinkle with sieved egg. Surround bowl of dip with potato or corn chips.

Makes about 1½ cups.

## AVOCADO COTTAGE DIP

Try out this uniquely flavored dip at your next party.

1½ cups small-curd cottage cheese
6 tablespoons dairy sour cream
1 small avocado, sieved or mashed
2 hard-cooked eggs, minced

1 tablespoon chopped sweet pickle
¼ cup minced bread-and-butter pickles
½ teaspoon salt
¼ teaspoon garlic salt
Dash pepper

Blend cottage cheese, sour cream, and avocado. Combine eggs, pickles, seasonings and add to avocado-cottage cheese mixture. Chill until time to serve.

Makes 2 cups.

## AVOCADO CRUNCHY DIP

Crisp, chopped, roasted almonds provide the delightful crunch
to this dip.

1 medium-sized avocado
1½ tablespoons fresh lemon or
    lime juice
Few drops Tabasco sauce
1½ teaspoons grated onion

Dash pepper
Dash cayenne
⅓ cup finely chopped
    roasted almonds

Sieve avocado; add remaining ingredients and blend thoroughly.
Use as dip with crackers, crisp celery sticks, or carrot strips.
Makes about 1 cup.

## AVOCADO SEAFOOD DIP

This is a dip that can double as a delicious sandwich spread.

1 large avocado
1 teaspoon salt
2 tablespoons lemon or lime juice
Few drops Tabasco sauce

Sieve avocado and blend in remaining ingredients. Serve as a
dip for cooked shrimp.
Makes 1 cup.

## AVOCADO TUNA DIP

Chances are you will be pleased with this flavor combination.

1 medium-sized avocado
1 cup small-curd cottage
   cheese
2 3-ounce packages cream
   cheese
2 teaspoons grated onion
½ cup tuna, drained and
   flaked

Dash cayenne
½ teaspoon salt
¼ teaspoon garlic salt
1 teaspoon lemon juice
4 tablespoons sour cream

Sieve avocado and blend together with cottage cheese, cream cheese, and onion. Add tuna, seasonings, and sour cream; blend thoroughly. Chill before serving.

Makes 2 cups.

## AVOCUMBER DIP

This dip is as refreshing as it is flavorsome.

2 medium-sized avocados
2 tablespoons lemon juice
1 small cucumber, peeled,
   seeded, and minced

2 tablespoons chopped parsley
1 teaspoon salt
½ teaspoon crushed tarragon

Halve and seed avocados. Scoop out avocado pulp; retain half-shells. Sieve or mash fruit and mix with lemon juice. Mix with all other ingredients. Cover and chill. Put dip into avocado half-shells to serve with carrot or celery sticks or corn chips.

Makes 2 cups.

## CAPRI SHRIMP DIP

This is a new idea in dips, with avocado and seafood as ideal teammates.

1 medium-sized avocado
2 tablespoons lemon or lime
   juice
Dash garlic salt
1 teaspoon salt
2 tablespoons chopped
   pimiento
1 cup small-curd cottage
   cheese

1 5-ounce can small shrimp
   or 1 7-ounce can minced
   clams, drained
Lettuce leaves
Paprika
Minced parsley

Mash or sieve avocado; blend in lemon or lime juice, garlic salt, salt, and pimiento. Add cottage cheese and shrimp (or clams). Pile into bowl; surround with crisp lettuce leaves. Sprinkle dip with paprika and minced parsley for garnish.
Makes 1½ cups.

## CHILI AVOCADO DIP

How smooth and zesty can a dip be? Here's the answer.

1 tablespoon instant onion
2 tablespoons lemon or lime
   juice
1 large avocado
1 3-ounce package cream
   cheese

2 tablespoons finely chopped
   canned green chili
1 teaspoon salt

Combine instant onion with lemon or lime juice and let stand a few minutes. Sieve or mash avocado and mix with softened cream cheese, then add onion, chili, salt and mix well.
Makes 1⅓ cups.

## CRAB AVOCADO DIP

If you wish a gourmet dip, here's one that is sure to delight.

Garlic salt to taste
2 tablespoons lemon juice
3 tablespoons salad oil

1 medium-sized avocado,
sieved
1 5-ounce can crab meat

Combine garlic salt and lemon juice; gradually beat in oil until well blended and then add sieved avocado, mixing well. Shred crab meat and fold into the mixture.
Makes 1½ cups.

## CURRIED AVOCADO DIP

Welcome guests with a festive predinner dip like this.

2 medium-sized avocados
4 tablespoons lemon juice
2 slices crisp-cooked bacon,
  crumbled
½ teaspoon curry powder
½ teaspoon chili powder
Dash garlic salt

1 tablespoon grated onion
1 tablespoon mayonnaise
½ teaspoon Worcestershire
  sauce
Dash Tabasco sauce
Salt to taste

Scoop out most of avocado pulp from half-shells, leaving enough for them to hold their shape. Sprinkle them with 1 tablespoon lemon juice. Mash or sieve avocado pulp that was removed; add crumbled bacon and all remaining ingredients including 3 table-spoons lemon juice. Beat until smooth and heap into avocado half-shells for serving. Serve as dip with crackers, chips, tostadas, or small points of buttered rye toast.
Makes about 1½ cups.

## DIPSY DOODLE DIP

This flavorsome dip will prove to be a crowd pleaser.

*1 medium-sized avocado*
*½ teaspoon salt*
*½ teaspoon dry mustard*
*1 teaspoon Worcestershire*
*    sauce*
*2 tablespoons anchovy paste*
*3 tablespoons wine vinegar*

*3 tablespoons minced chives*
*    or 1 tablespoon grated*
*    onion*
*¼ cup minced parsley*
*1 cup mayonnaise*
*½ cup dairy sour cream*
*Dash pepper*

Mash or sieve avocado. Combine with all remaining ingredients and refrigerate until served as a dip for shrimp, lobster, chips, or any other dipper.
Makes 1½ cups.

## GUACAMOLE (pronounced Wah-kah-mó-lay)

Guacamole is an increasingly popular avocado dip. It is being used as a canapé spread, as an ingredient for hors d'oeuvres, or as a delicious dressing on ripe, red tomato slices as a salad. No one ever really follows one guacamole recipe, for there are as many ways of making it as there are people who make it. Guacamole can be made in advance and refrigerated until serving time and served either in an avocado half-shell or in a small serving bowl surrounded by a choice of "dippers."

## BASIC GUACAMOLE DIP

*2 to 3 medium-sized*
*    avocados*
*2 tablespoons lemon juice or*
*    1½ tablespoons wine*
*    vinegar*

*1 8-ounce package cream*
*    cheese*
*1½ teaspoons salt*
*¼ teaspoon chili powder*
*Dash Tabasco sauce*
*1 tablespoon grated onion*

*Tomato-Avocado Hors d'oeuvres.* Serve cocktail picks to spear cherry tomatoes and avocado balls for dip-dunking. (page 17)

*Guacamole Dip* gives you the answer as to how smooth a dip can be. (page 26)

1

*Fruit Cocktail.* A medley of fruits plus avocado provides a perfect cocktail combination. (page 31)

This goes to show you there is something new under the sun—guaca mole on a piping hot ear of corn. (page 26)

*Piquant Cocktail*, delicately flavored avocado half-shells filled with canned artichoke hearts, is served with a nippy sauce. (page 41)

*Avocado Soup, Delmonico,* is a tomato-avocado soup that may be served hot or cold. (page 47)

Mash or sieve avocados. Blend in all remaining ingredients. Refrigerate until ready to serve as a dip.*

Makes 1–2 cups.

VARIATIONS:

*Bacon:* Fold in ¼ cup finely crumbled crisp bacon.

*Cheese:* Fold in ¼ cup finely crumbled Roquefort cheese.

*Chives:* Omit onion and fold in 1 to 2 tablespoons finely minced chives.

*Cottage cheese:* Substitute 8 ounces or ½ cup small-curd cottage cheese for cream cheese.

*Deviled ham:* Fold in ¼ cup deviled ham.

*Egg:* Fold in ¼ cup finely chopped cooked egg.

*Green pepper:* Omit Tabasco sauce or chili powder; fold in 2 to 3 tablespoons chopped green pepper or canned green chili peppers.

*Pickle:* Fold in ¼ cup finely chopped dill pickle or well-drained sweet pickle relish.

*Pimiento:* Fold in 2 to 3 tablespoons finely chopped pimiento.

## PARTY AVOCADO DIP

Here's a dip that is so velvety, delicious, and tantalizing!

| | |
|---|---|
| 1 medium-sized avocado, sieved | 1 teaspoon salt |
| | ½ teaspoon grated onion |
| 2 tablespoons lemon or lime juice | Tabasco sauce |
| | ⅓ cup diced smoked tongue |

Blend sieved avocado with remaining ingredients. Refrigerate until ready to use as a dip or spread.

Makes about ⅔ cup.

* FRESH-FROZEN: Get Avocado Dip (Guacamole) from Frozen Food section of the supermarket. Thaw and if desired add any other ingredients desired just before serving.

## PIP OF A DIP

These unusual ingredients will keep guests guessing.

2 medium-sized avocados
¼ cup lemon juice
Garlic salt to taste
½ cup cooked mashed
  potatoes

1 teaspoon chicken stock*
½ teaspoon salt
2 tablespoons chopped chives
2 tablespoons chopped parsley

Sieve avocados; add few drops of lemon juice. Combine all remaining ingredients and blend together with the avocado. Refrigerate until serving time.

Makes about 2 cups.

## SHRIMP DIP

Avocado balls and shrimp dipped into a tangy sauce are perfect!

½ cup chili sauce
2 tablespoons lemon juice
1 tablespoon horseradish
  (optional)
1 teaspoon grated onion
1 teaspoon Worcestershire
  sauce

Dash Tabasco sauce
2 medium-sized avocados
Salt to taste
1 cup or 1 5-ounce can
  medium-sized shrimp

Combine all ingredients except avocados, salt, and shrimp and chill. Halve, seed, and peel avocados and cut into balls; sprinkle with salt. Arrange avocado balls and shrimp on platter and set out cocktail picks for spearing them and dipping them into the tangy sauce.

Makes ¾ cup.

* Or 1 chicken bouillon cube softened in 1 tablespoon water.

## "QUICKIE" IDEAS

*Continental Dip:* For an interesting dip to serve with hot meat balls, combine mashed avocado with lemon juice, sour cream, a little prepared mustard, and instant onion or onion salt. It's different and delicious.

*Popular Dip:* To mashed avocado seasoned with salt, add instant minced onion or onion salt and lemon juice; combine with a small can of deviled ham.

*Clam Dip:* Mash avocado and blend in a small can of drained minced clams. Season with salt, pepper, lemon juice, dash of onion salt, and Tabasco sauce.

*Salmon Dip:* Cut avocado into bite-sized cubes. Dip in Mayonnaise thinned with lemon juice; roll cubes in crushed potato chips or dip cubes in lemon juice and wrap each with a thin strip of smoked salmon or dried beef. Serve on a cocktail toothpick.

*Shrimp Dippers:* Mix crumbled bacon, instant onion, lemon juice, and salt with mashed avocado. Use large shrimp as "dippers" instead of crackers or chips.

## COCKTAILS

### *Fruit Cocktails*

Fruit cocktails make a delightful meal starter, a fact too often overlooked. The smooth, delicious edibility and attractive cool, green tint of avocados are never in better setting than in combination with other fruits. The effect is heightened by serving them in elegant, chilled glassware or, by way of change, in avocado half-shells. Portions should be conservative; the taste a bit on the sharp side, not too bland or sweet. The hostess must always keep in mind that the cocktail is only the beginning of the meal.

## AUTUMN COCKTAIL

You will approve of the lemon-honey dressing for this cocktail.

1 medium-sized avocado
1 cup sliced bananas
1½ cups sliced seedless
    grapes

Lemon-Honey Dressing
(given below)

Cut avocado into small cubes and combine with other prepared fruits. Put in chilled cocktail glasses or fruit cups. Serve with lemon-honey dressing.

*Lemon-Honey Dressing:* Combine equal portions of lemon juice and honey and blend thoroughly.

Makes 5 to 6 servings.

## AVOCADO CRANBERRY FROST COCKTAIL

Here is an unusual fruit cocktail par excellence.

1 large avocado
¾ cup diced pineapple

SAUCE:

½ cup sugar
1 cup water
1 cup uncooked cranberries

Cut avocado into cubes. Arrange alternately with pineapple cubes in cocktail glasses. Add sauce just before serving.

*Sauce:* Combine sugar, water, and cranberries; boil about 5 minutes. Remove from heat and rub through a sieve. Chill.

Makes 4 to 5 servings.

## AVOCADO FRUIT COCKTAIL

Lead off the meal with this distinctive cocktail.

2 *large avocados*
4 *cups grapefruit segments*
  (*canned may be used*)
2 *cups orange pieces*
2 *cups sliced, sweetened*
  *strawberries*

1½ *cups honey*
1½ *cups lemon or lime juice*
2 *cups pineapple juice*

Cut avocados into balls; combine with other fruits, honey, lemon or lime and pineapple juices. Serve well chilled.
Makes 16 servings.

## AVOCADO SUNSET COCKTAIL

For an appetizer, you'll be proud to serve this one.

1 *medium-sized avocado*
2 *cups canned peach slices*
1 *cup syrup from peaches*

¼ *cup maraschino cherry*
  *syrup*
¼ *cup lemon or lime juice*
¼ *teaspoon lemon rind*

Cut avocado into cubes. Dice peaches and combine all fruits. Put in chilled fruit cups. Blend syrups, juice, and rind and pour over fruits. Serve very cold.
Makes 6 servings.

## CALIFORNIA SUNSHINE CUP

You want just the perfect Christmas dinner starter, and here is one of the best.

1 *large avocado*
2 8-*ounce cans grapefruit*
  *sections*

1 *cup seeded red grapes,*
  *sliced*
½ *cup sherry*
*Dash Angostura bitters*

Cut avocado into cubes or balls. Cut grapefruit into bite-sized sections; seed and slice grapes. Combine all fruits with wine and bitters and serve in stemmed cocktail glasses.

Makes 6 servings.

## CELEBRITY AVOCADO COCKTAIL

This combination should stimulate any lagging appetites.

*2 medium-sized avocados,*
  *balled or cubed*
*1 cup seeded, halved grapes*
*½ cup canned cling peaches,*
  *sliced*

*½ cup thawed frozen or*
  *fresh strawberries*
*1 cup syrup from peaches*
*Lime or lemon juice*
*Honey*

Combine avocado balls or cubes, grapes, peaches, and strawberries in fruit cups. Blend peach syrup with lime or lemon juice and honey to taste and pour over fruits.

Makes 5 to 6 servings.

## CLAREMONT COCKTAIL

Here is a cocktail that features avocado seasoned to a queen's taste.

*¼ cup chili sauce*
*¼ cup mayonnaise*
*1 tablespoon lemon or lime*
  *juice*

*1 teaspoon horseradish*
*¼ cup table cream*
*1 large avocado, cubed or*
  *diced*

Blend together chili sauce, mayonnaise, lemon or lime juice, horseradish, and cream. Place cubed or diced avocado into 4 or 5 fruit cups; pour chilled sauce over avocado.

Makes 4 to 5 servings.

## FESTIVE AVOCADO COCKTAIL

A red and green cocktail is in perfect keeping with Christmas holidays.

2 medium-sized avocados
¼ cup finely diced celery
½ cup cooked whole
   cranberries or canned
   cranberry sauce
½ cup chopped unpeeled red
   apples

⅓ cup honey
2 tablespoons lemon or lime
   juice
¾ cup chilled fruit juice

Cube avocados; combine with celery, cranberries, and apples in stemmed glasses. Blend honey and lemon or lime juice and add to chilled fruit juice of your choice. Pour over fruits and serve cold.

Makes 6 servings.

## FROSTY FRUIT CUP

This unusual cocktail combines apricot nectar and avocado.

1 cup apricot fruit nectar
Fresh lemon or lime juice
1 large avocado

Blend nectar and 2 tablespoons lemon or lime juice. Put in freezing compartment for 1 to 1½ hours, until mushy. Stir occasionally with a fork. Cube avocado; sprinkle with lemon juice. Arrange in 4 chilled sherbet glasses and top with the frozen nectar.

Makes 4 servings.

## FRUITS MONTEREY

Excellent for a predinner fruit cup, dessert, or luncheon nut bread sandwiches, cold milk or iced tea.

*1 large avocado, cubed or balled*
*1 cup diced orange sections*
*1 cup pitted fresh or canned cherries*
*1½ cups chilled fruit juice (any)*

*Sugar to taste*
*3 tablespoons lemon or lime juice*
*¼ teaspoon grated lemon or lime rind*

Combine avocado cubes or balls with other fruits. Blend chilled fruit juice, sugar, lemon or lime juice, and rind; pour over fruits. Makes 4 to 6 servings.

## IMPERIAL MELON AVOCADO COCKTAIL

Almost everyone likes a cocktail with a surprise flavor, and this one has it.

*1 large avocado, balled*
*2 tablespoons lemon juice*
*1 cup Persian, Crenshaw, or any other melon of choice, balled*
*1 cup tomato juice*

*1 tablespoon tomato catsup*
*1 teaspoon grated onion*
*½ teaspoon sugar*
*Dash Tabasco sauce*
*Salt to taste*
*Mint or parsley*

Roll avocado balls in lemon juice. Put avocado and melon balls into fruit cups. Mix rest of ingredients and pour over fruit balls. Serve very cold garnished with sprig of mint or parsley. Makes 4 servings.

## SANTA BARBARA FRUIT COCKTAIL

Velvety-smooth avocado and cherries combine to make a delicious fruit cup.

1 medium-sized avocado          2 tablespoons lemon juice
1 cup fresh or canned Royal     ¼ cup grenadine syrup
   Anne cherries

Cube avocado and pit cherries. Arrange equal parts into cocktail glasses. Blend juice, grenadine syrup and pour over fruit. Makes 3 to 4 servings.

## SIERRA FRUIT CUP

Lead into the meal with this delectable fruit medley cocktail.

1 medium-sized avocado,         ½ cup fresh berries (any)
   cubed                        ⅓ cup honey
½ cup canned cling peach        ¼ cup lemon or lime juice
   slices                       ¼ teaspoon grated lemon or
½ cup fresh or canned pears        lime rind
½ cup orange sections           1 cup orange juice

Combine cubed avocado with other fruits, which have been diced, and arrange equally in fruit cups. Blend remaining ingredients and pour over fruits. Serve well chilled. Makes 6 servings.

## *Seafood Cocktails*

Smart, sophisticated, and welcome is the custom of serving seafood cocktails as a first dinner course. When seafood is combined with avocado and a zesty dressing, the "just right" flavor and color combination are achieved.

## ALASKA SALMON COCKTAIL

Crisp cheese wafers go well with this pink-green cocktail.

*1 large avocado, cubed*
*Fresh lemon or lime juice*
*Salt*
*1 7½-ounce can salmon*
*½ cup mayonnaise*

*3 tablespoons French dressing*
*1 tablespoon prepared*
  *mustard*
*½ cup tomato catsup*
*Crushed potato chips*

Sprinkle avocado cubes with lemon or lime juice and salt. Combine with drained, flaked salmon and arrange in 6 cocktail glasses. Blend mayonnaise, French dressing, mustard, catsup and pour over salmon-avocado mixture. Just before serving, sprinkle top of each cocktail with finely crushed potato chips.
Makes 6 servings.

## AVOCADO CLAM COCKTAIL

Here's a subtle flavor combination your holiday guests will applaud.

*1 medium-sized avocado*
*2 tablespoons diced tomato*
*1 tablespoon grated onion*
*2 tablespoons finely diced*
  *celery*
*Salt to taste*
*¼ cup minced clams,*
  *undrained*

*2 tablespoons tomato catsup*
*1 tablespoon lemon juice*
*Dash Tabasco sauce*
*Dash Worcestershire sauce*
*⅛ teaspoon horseradish*

Cube avocado and blend with tomato, onion, and celery. Sprinkle lightly with salt. Divide into 5 or 6 cocktail glasses. Blend remaining ingredients and pour over the avocado mixture. Chill.
Makes 5 to 6 servings.

## HARBOR AVOCADO COCKTAIL

Tuna and avocado are a congenial twosome.

¾ cup tomato cocktail sauce
3 tablespoons mayonnaise
Dash Tabasco sauce
1 teaspoon lemon or lime juice
1 tablespoon sweet pickle
  relish

2 tablespoons French dressing
1 6-ounce can tuna, flaked
1 medium-sized avocado,
  cubed
¼ cup finely chopped celery
¼ cup chopped green pepper

Combine cocktail sauce, mayonnaise, Tabasco sauce, lemon or lime juice, pickle relish, and French dressing thoroughly. Lightly stir in flaked tuna, avocado cubes, celery, and green pepper. Serve well chilled. Makes 4 servings.

## MANHATTAN CRAB COCKTAIL

Here's an elegant savory cocktail treat!

1 medium-sized avocado
1 7½-ounce can crab meat,
  flaked
1½ cups fresh tomatoes,
  diced

½ cup finely chopped celery
2 tablespoons lemon or lime
  juice
Salt to taste
⅔ cup seafood cocktail sauce

Cube avocado; combine with crab meat, tomatoes, celery, lemon or lime juice and salt to taste. Spoon into cocktail glasses and top with chilled cocktail sauce just before serving.
Makes 6 to 8 servings.

## MONTEREY SHRIMP COCKTAIL

Add mellow-flavored avocado to shrimp to have an extra special cocktail.

| | |
|---|---|
| 1 large avocado | 2 tablespoons lemon juice |
| Salt | Dash Worcestershire sauce |
| 1 4½-ounce can shrimp | Dash Tabasco sauce |
| ⅓ cup tomato catsup | ½ cup finely chopped celery |

Cut avocado into cubes; sprinkle with salt. Add shrimp. Blend remaining ingredients and pour over cubed avocado and shrimp. Makes 4 servings.

## SAN JUAN COCKTAIL

This cocktail serves as a salad as well as a cocktail.

| | |
|---|---|
| 2 medium-sized avocados | ½ cup catsup |
| Fresh lemon juice | ¼ cup mayonnaise |
| Salt | 2 teaspoons lemon or lime |
| 1 7½-ounce can minced | juice |
| clams, drained | Dash Tabasco sauce |
| ⅓ cup finely cut celery | Cracked ice or salad greens |

Cut avocados in half lengthwise; retain the shells after removing the fruit. Sprinkle half-shells with a little lemon juice and salt. Cut removed fruit into cubes and combine with drained clams, celery, catsup, mayonnaise, lemon or lime juice and Tabasco sauce. Fill avocado half-shells with avocado-clam mixture. Serve in bowl of cracked ice or on salad greens as a salad.
Makes 6 servings.

## Vegetable Cocktails

Avocados prove their versatility when combined with well-selected ingredients such as many varieties of vegetables.

### AVOCADO RELISH COCKTAIL

Impress guests with this unusual cocktail as a starter course.

| | |
|---|---|
| 1 medium-sized avocado | ½ teaspoon salt |
| 1 cup finely cut celery | 2 teaspoons prepared mustard |
| ¾ cup chopped green pepper | 2 tablespoons mayonnaise |
| ¼ cup lemon or lime juice | 2 tablespoons sweet pickle |
| ¼ cup salad oil | relish |
| 2 tablespoons sugar | |

Cube the avocado and combine with celery and pepper. Combine the remaining ingredients except mayonnaise and pickle relish and add to the avocado mixture. Before serving, top each cocktail with a mixture of the mayonnaise and pickle relish.

Makes 4 to 6 servings.

### AVOCADO ROQUEFORT COCKTAIL

Cheese and avocado are ingredients that make this cocktail distinctive.

| | |
|---|---|
| 1 medium-sized avocado | 1 teaspoon grated onion |
| Lemon or lime juice | Dash Tabasco sauce |
| Salt | 2 tablespoons Roquefort |
| ⅓ cup finely chopped celery | cheese, crumbled |
| ¼ cup tomato catsup | Parsley |
| 2 tablespoons lemon juice | |

Cube avocado and sprinkle with a little lemon or lime juice and salt. Blend lightly with celery and put into 4 cocktail glasses. Combine remaining ingredients except parsley and pour over avocado-celery mixture. Garnish with a sprig of parsley.

Makes 4 servings.

## AVOCADO TOMATO COCKTAIL

Filled avocado half-shells are unusual, pretty, and appealing.

2 medium-sized avocados
Lemon or lime juice
Salt
1 cup finely chopped celery
¼ cup chopped ripe olives

⅔ cup tomato cocktail sauce
⅓ cup mayonnaise
1 tablespoon lemon juice
Dash Tabasco sauce
Cracked ice or salad greens

Cut avocados in half lengthwise; sprinkle with lemon or lime juice and salt. Fill half-shells with celery. Combine remaining ingredients, blending well. Pour mixture over filled avocado shells. Serve in bowl of cracked ice or on salad greens as individual salads.
Makes 4 servings.

## BEST-EVER AVOCADO COCKTAIL

Sharp, appetite-stimulating, and easy to prepare is this cocktail.

1 medium-sized avocado
½ cup finely chopped celery
½ cup cooked mixed
   vegetables
1 tablespoon finely minced
   onion

¼ teaspoon salt
1 tablespoon lemon juice
3 tablespoons chili sauce
Dash Worcestershire sauce

Cube avocado and combine with remaining ingredients, tossing lightly. Arrange in cocktail glasses; chill well before serving.
Makes 4 servings.

## LUCERNE AVOCADO COCKTAIL

This unusual cocktail will really whet the appetite.

1 medium-sized avocado
Lemon juice
Salt
Dash Worcestershire sauce
½ teaspoon grated onion
⅓ cup tomato catsup

½ teaspoon prepared
    horseradish
¼ cup grated carrot
1 tablespoon lemon juice
1 tablespoon vinegar

Cube avocado and sprinkle with lemon juice and salt. Combine remaining ingredients and pour over avocado. Chill and serve. Makes 4 servings.

## PIQUANT COCKTAIL

Here is a cocktail that lives up to its name!

2 to 3 medium-sized
    avocados
2 tablespoons lemon or lime
    juice
Salt

1 cup canned artichoke
    hearts, diced
⅔ cup tomato cocktail sauce
⅓ cup mayonnaise
Dash Tabasco sauce
Cracked ice

Cut avocados in half lengthwise and sprinkle half-shells with 1 tablespoon lemon or lime juice and a little salt. Fill shells with artichoke hearts and top with blended cocktail sauce, 1 tablespoon lemon or lime juice, mayonnaise, and Tabasco sauce. Serve in bowl of cracked ice.
Makes 4 to 6 servings.

## RAINBOW COCKTAIL

You may be looking for a very unusual cocktail and this is one.

1 10½-ounce can beef
    consommé
⅓ cup finely diced
    cucumber
½ pint dairy sour cream
¼ teaspoon salt

Dash pepper
1 medium-sized avocado
2 tablespoons lemon juice
¼ teaspoon onion salt
Parsley

Pour consommé into 6 wine or parfait glasses. Chill several hours until firm. Mix cucumber, sour cream, salt and pepper and spoon over the jellied consommé. Sieve avocado and mix with lemon juice, and onion salt. Put avocado mixture on top of the cucumber mixture. Garnish with sprig of parsley.

Makes 6 servings.


## "QUICKIE" IDEAS

*Fruit Medley:* To start off company meals, serve an avocado half-shell with pink grapefruit sections and halved, seeded grapes in the center. Top with a lemon juice and oil dressing flavored with a little celery seed.

*Do-It-Yourself Cocktail:* Serve an avocado half-shell with a wedge of fresh lime. Gash fruit with edge of a spoon; sprinkle on a little sugar. Squeeze on lime juice and let the sugar-lime mixture run down into the cuts. This is the South American way!

# *Soups*

"Soup of the evening, beautiful soup!"
—Lewis Carroll, *Alice in Wonderland*

Good soup is considered to be one of the prime ingredients of good living, and if true, the addition of avocado to soups makes living even better, makes an ordinary soup into one that is extra special. It is doubtful that even imaginative cooks have realized until recent times that the attractive and nutritional qualities of the avocado could be utilized in soup-making. Today, there need be no involvement of long hours of preparation, tedious efforts, and the use of many ingredients in order to achieve a soup par excellence. Avocado soups are surprisingly easy to prepare, require little time and few ingredients. One important thing to remember in preparing avocado soups is that the heating of avocado accentuates its flavor, but actually cooking avocado will destroy the delicate flavor. The steamy fragrance of a bowl of elegant, creamy, avocado soup for luncheon, supper, brunch, or dinner provides the "just right" welcome to the meal or main dish that is to follow. Next time you are entertaining, serve an avocado soup as a conversation piece!

## AVOCADO BOUILLON

Avocado as an ingredient in soup is sure to evoke surprise.

1 10½-ounce can chicken
   bouillon or broth
1 soup can water
¼ cup clam juice (optional)
1 medium-sized avocado
Salt to taste

2 tablespoons sherry or lemon
   juice
½ cup whipping cream,
   whipped
Parsley
Paprika

Combine bouillon or broth, water, and clam juice if used. Heat piping hot. Meanwhile cube avocado and spoon cubes into each bouillon cup or soup bowl. Sprinkle a little salt on the cubes. Just before serving add sherry or lemon juice to the hot broth. Pour broth over the avocado cubes. Top each bowl of broth with a small dollop of whipped cream and garnish with a bit of minced parsley and paprika. Serve immediately with thin, salted crackers.

Makes 4 to 6 servings.

## AVOCADO CELERY SOUP

Start off the next dinner party with this delicious avocado soup.

| | |
|---|---|
| ¼ cup finely chopped onion | 1 cup table cream |
| ½ cup finely sliced celery | 1 teaspoon salt |
| 1 tablespoon butter | 1 medium-sized avocado |
| 1 cup milk | |

Sauté onion and celery in butter about 5 minutes. Add milk, cream, salt and heat to boiling point. Remove from heat and stir in sieved or mashed avocado. Serve at once.

Makes 4 servings.

## AVOCADO CHICKEN SOUP

Try an appetizing chicken soup with a new flavor.

| | |
|---|---|
| 2 cups chicken broth | 1 medium-sized avocado |
| 1 cup milk | 2 teaspoons grated onion |
| 2 tablespoons flour | |

Heat chicken broth to boiling. Make a thin paste of ¼ cup milk and 2 tablespoons flour, then add ¾ cup of milk. Add the paste slowly to the chicken broth and bring to boil again. Add sieved or mashed avocado and stir in onion. Heat through but do not boil; serve immediately.

Makes 4 servings.

## AVOCADO CURRY SOUP

Extra special is the term for this soup.

1 tablespoon butter
1 teaspoon curry
1 can condensed chicken
   consommé

1 cup table cream
1 slightly beaten egg yolk
1 medium-sized avocado

Melt butter, stir in curry and add consommé. Bring to boil; cover and simmer 10 minutes. Combine cream with egg yolk and gradually stir into the soup. Mash half of the avocado; dice the other half; add both to the soup. Heat, stirring constantly. Serve hot or cold.

Makes 4 to 5 servings.

## AVOCADO MUSHROOM SOUP

This soup makes an elegant beginning for any dinner.

1 tablespoon butter
1 tablespoon chopped onion
1 4-ounce can sliced
   mushrooms

3 cups chicken broth
2 tablespoons cornstarch
Salt and pepper to taste
1 large avocado, diced

Melt butter; add onion and cook about 5 minutes. Drain mushrooms, reserving liquid. Add mushrooms to onion and cook together about 1 minute. Blend broth with cornstarch and mushroom liquid. Add onion-mushroom mixture to broth and heat until thickened. Season to taste. Just before serving, add the diced avocado.

Makes 8 servings.

## AVOCADO SEA-BREEZE SOUP

Prepare this fresh-tasting soup for a hot summer's day luncheon.

*1 medium-sized avocado*          *Dairy sour cream*
*2 cups buttermilk*               *Paprika*
*½ teaspoon salt*
*1 10-ounce can frozen*
*condensed clam chowder,*
*unthawed*

Put avocado into blender; add buttermilk, salt, and the un-thawed clam chowder. Whirl in blender until mixture is smoothly blended, then serve. If no blender is used, mash the avocado and beat into the thawed chowder, buttermilk, and salt. Garnish with a small dollop of sour cream and paprika.
Makes 6 servings.

## AVOCADO SHERRY SOUP

This will be the surprise course of the luncheon or dinner.

*2 medium-sized avocados*          *3 tablespoons sherry*
*3 cups chicken stock or broth*    *Salt and pepper to taste*
*1½ cups table cream*

Mash or sieve 1½ avocados and combine with the chicken broth and cream. Heat the soup just to the boiling point; stir in sherry, salt and pepper. Cut other half of avocado into cubes or balls and drop into the soup just before serving.
Makes 6 servings.

## AVOCADO SOUP, DELMONICO

This delectable clear soup may be served hot or cold.

6 medium-sized firm, fresh
  tomatoes
6 green onions
1 small clove garlic or
  garlic salt to taste
6 peppercorns
1 teaspoon salt
1 teaspoon sugar

1 bay leaf
3 beef bouillon cubes
3 cups boiling water
1 medium-sized avocado,
  sliced
Lemon or lime wedges
  (optional)

Wash, cut up tomatoes and onions. Mince garlic. Add pepper-corns, salt, sugar, and bay leaf and simmer together 20 to 30 minutes. Dissolve bouillon cubes in boiling water. Strain tomato mixture into bouillon. Simmer 15 minutes. Chill. Just before serving, float thin avocado slices on top of soup servings. Serve with little lime or lemon wedges, if desired.

Makes 6 servings.

## FIESTA AVOCADO SOUP

For that festive occasion, why not serve this soup?

1 medium-sized avocado
¼ cup finely chopped onion
½ cup thinly sliced celery
1 tablespoon butter or
  margarine

1 cup milk
1 cup table cream
1 teaspoon salt
1 hard-cooked egg, sieved

Mash or sieve avocado. Cook onion and celery in butter or margarine slowly until tender. Add milk, cream, and salt; heat to boiling. Remove from heat and stir in sieved avocado slowly; serve at once. Garnish with a thin slice of avocado topped with sieved hard-cooked egg.

Makes 4 servings.

## GINGER AVOCADO SOUP

Connoisseurs will approve of this soup.

*¼ cup butter or margarine*
*¼ cup flour*
*1 quart milk*
*2 teaspoons salt*
*¼ teaspoon powdered ginger*
*1½ teaspoons grated orange*
  *rind*

*2 medium-sized avocados*
*½ cup whipping cream,*
  *whipped*
*1 tablespoon finely chopped*
  *preserved ginger*

Melt butter or margarine in saucepan; blend in flour, then milk, stirring constantly until mixture thickens. Stir in salt, powdered ginger, and orange rind. Remove from heat. Sieve avocados; add to soup. Return to heat; gently heat through but do not boil. Serve hot or chilled with a dollop of whipped cream and a sprinkling of preserved ginger.

Makes 6 to 8 servings.


## GREEN ISLE AVOCADO SOUP

Here is a soup worthy of any gourmet luncheon or dinner.

*2 medium-sized avocados*
*¾ cup whipping cream*
*Onion salt*

*Pepper*
*1½ quarts concentrated*
  *chicken stock*

Whip the avocado pulp into a paste. Add whipping cream and continue to whip until rather stiff. Add a pinch each of onion salt and pepper. Bring chicken broth to a boil and carefully add the avocado mixture to the hot broth. Serve at once.

Makes 8 servings.

## NOB HILL AVOCADO SOUP

This is an aristocratic soup in the San Francisco tradition.

*1 tablespoon minced onion*
*3 tablespoons butter or*
  *margarine*
*3 tablespoons flour*
*1 quart milk*
*2 chicken bouillon cubes*

*1 cup diced cooked chicken*
*Dash pepper*
*Salt to taste*
*1 large avocado*
*1 tablespoon lemon or lime*
  *juice*

Cook onion slowly in butter or margarine until lightly browned. Blend in flour; stir in milk. Add bouillon cubes, diced chicken, seasonings. Cook and stir until mixture thickens. Sieve avocado; blend with lemon or lime juice. Just before serving, pour hot mixture slowly over avocado, stirring until well blended. Serve at once.

Makes 6 to 8 servings.

## SHRIMP AVOCADO BISQUE

Present this soup to your sophisticated friends.

*1 tablespoon instant minced*
  *onion*
*2 10½-ounce cans cream of*
  *chicken or mushroom soup*
*2 cups milk*

*1 tablespoon butter*
*1 cup cleaned, cooked shrimp*
*2 tablespoons diced pimiento*
*1 large avocado*

Combine instant onion and canned soup. Add milk gradually and stir until mixture is smooth. Heat and add butter, shrimp, and pimiento. Dice avocado; drop into soup and heat about 2 minutes only. Serve immediately.

Makes 6 servings.

## VICHYSSOISE À LA AVOCADO

This soup is twice as pretty and appetizing as the usual vichyssoise.

*1 10½-ounce can cream of potato soup*
*½ soup can milk*
*½ soup can cream*
*½ teaspoon grated onion*

*1 medium-sized avocado, sieved*
*Salt and pepper to taste*
*Dash curry powder*
*Chives or parsley*

Heat cream of potato soup with milk and cream; add grated onion. Cool, then blend in sieved avocado. Add seasonings and continue beating, either in an electric blender or with rotary beater until mixture is very smooth. Chill 4 hours or more and serve in chilled bowls. Sprinkle with finely minced chives or minced parsley.
Makes 5 servings.

## "QUICKIE" IDEAS

Add mashed or sieved avocados to either cream soups of almost any kind or wafer-thin slices of avocado to any clear soup, just before serving.

Mash 1 avocado with juice of ½ lemon. Season with choice of herbs. Add dash of salt and 1 can jellied beef consommé. Beat until smooth. Soup will be thick. Thin with water or thicken in refrigerator for half hour. Ideal for hot day luncheon.

Combine 2 11-ounce cans condensed chili-beef soup with 2 soup cans water; heat, stirring occasionally, and top with generous dollop of guacamole (see Index).

*Jellied Consommé in Avocado:* Spoon a well-chilled can 10½-ounce consommé into 6 avocado half-shells. Garnish with dollop of sour cream and little grated onion and serve in small bowls lined with lettuce. Good for a summer day luncheon.

*Dieter's Special.* Here is a luncheon special having a minimum of calories and a maximum of nutritive values.

*Salad—Unmolded (Fruit).* A salad with a variety of fruits is made to order for a special occasion or the family menu.

5

# Salads and Salad Dressings

"Ho! 'Tis the time of salads."
—Laurence Sterne, *Tristram Shandy*

There is an ever-increasing demand for salads of all kinds and a greater awareness of their contribution to health as well as gastronomical enjoyment. The type of salad, and when it is served, is an important consideration; whether it is to be a complement to a meal or a whole meal in itself.

The custom of serving salad as a first course at dinner seems to have originated in the West and Southwest. People from other places appeared to like the idea and adopted it, so that a hostess anywhere may serve a salad course before dinner if she prefers it that way.

Salads may be divided into two main categories: molded and unmolded. Molded salads are prime company fare, are attractive and easy to prepare. An added advantage is that they are prepared ahead of time, whisked out of the refrigerator at the last minute before serving time. The unmolded salad consists of a variety of many ingredients tastefully tossed together or elaborately arranged in designs on salad plates.

The avocado is a natural salad ingredient for both molded and unmolded salads, since it blends so admirably with all other salad ingredients: fruits, vegetables, meats, poultry, or seafoods. When an avocado is cut in half and the seed removed, the perfect little hollows make inviting cups. Fill them up!

## MOLDED SALADS

Molded salads, whether sweet, tart, or fancy, give a festive look to the luncheon or dinner table. The avocado lends itself especially well to molded salads because of its mellow flavor, which never overpowers the flavor of other ingredients, its smoothness of texture, and its cool, delicate green color. When you are having a party, have molded salads with color, luxurious garnishes, and molded in fancy shapes to suit the occasion or the season. The prettiest salad plates should be selected to serve as a worthy background for that fabulous salad you wish all to enjoy.

## Molded Fruit Salads

### AURORA SALAD MOLDS

Try this refreshing combination of avocado with pimiento and pineapple.

| | |
|---|---|
| 1 3-ounce package lime gelatin | 1 8¼-ounce can crushed pineapple |
| 1¼ cups hot water | Few grains salt |
| 3 tablespoons fresh lemon juice | 1 large avocado, diced |
| | 2 tablespoons diced pimiento |

Dissolve gelatin in hot water. Blend in lemon juice, pineapple, and salt. Cool until slightly thickened. Fold diced avocado and pimiento into gelatin mixture. Turn into individual molds and chill until firm.
Makes 6 servings.

### AVOCADO CASHEW SQUARES

It would be difficult to find a salad with a more enchanting tropical flavor.

| | |
|---|---|
| 2 3-ounce packages lime gelatin | 1 medium-sized avocado, sliced |
| 3¾ cups hot water | ¾ cup cashew nuts |
| ¼ cup lemon juice | |

Dissolve gelatin in hot water. Add lemon juice and pour half of gelatin into 8-inch square pan. Chill until slightly thickened. Place avocado slices over gelatin in pan. Add cashew nuts and pour in remaining gelatin. Chill until firm. Cut in squares and serve.
Makes 8 servings.

## AVOCADO COCKTAIL MOLD

All guests should approve of this eye-appealing fruit salad.

*1 3-ounce package lemon*
*gelatin*
*1¼ cups hot water*
*½ cup syrup from fruit*
*cocktail*
*2 tablespoons fresh lemon*
*juice*

*Few grains salt*
*1 medium-sized avocado,*
*cubed*
*1 17-ounce can fruit cocktail*

Dissolve gelatin in hot water. Blend in fruit cocktail syrup, lemon juice, and salt. Chill until slightly thickened. Combine avocado and fruit cocktail and fold into gelatin. Turn into mold. Chill until firm. Unmold.
Makes 6 servings.

## AVOCADO CRANBERRY SALAD

Keep this salad in mind for holiday meals.

*1 3-ounce package lemon*
*gelatin*
*1½ cups hot water*
*3 tablespoons fresh lemon*
*juice*

*¼ teaspoon salt*
*2 medium-sized avocados,*
*cubed*
*1 cup sweetened cooked*
*whole cranberries*

Dissolve gelatin in hot water and stir in lemon juice and salt. Chill until slightly thickened. Whip chilled thickened gelatin until light and frothy. Fold avocados and well-drained cranberries into gelatin. Pour into mold. Chill until firm. Unmold.
Makes 6 to 8 servings.

## AVOCADO GRAPE MOLDS

Don't forget this salad for that next festive occasion.

1 3-ounce package lemon
  gelatin
1¾ cups hot water
3 tablespoons fresh lemon
  juice
2 medium-sized avocados,
  cubed

Salt
1 cup halved seeded grapes
¼ cup halved blanched
  almonds

Dissolve gelatin in hot water. Stir in lemon juice and cool until slightly thickened. Sprinkle avocados with salt. Add avocados, grapes, and almonds to gelatin, and blend lightly. Pour into 6 individual molds and chill until firm. Unmold.
Makes 6 servings.

## AVOCADO JEWEL SALAD

Here's a lovely fruit mixture for a salad.

1 envelope plain gelatin
¼ cup cold water
1 cup hot water
¼ cup fresh lemon juice
3 tablespoons sugar

½ teaspoon salt
1 medium-sized avocado,
  cubed
½ cup diced red apple
½ cup cubed orange sections

Soften gelatin in cold water and dissolve in hot water. Blend in lemon juice, sugar, and salt, and chill until slightly thickened. Fold avocado, apple, and orange into gelatin mixture. Pour into mold. Chill until firm.
Makes 6 servings.

## AVOCADO LYRIC SALADS

If you are looking for a refreshing salad for a warm day, try this one.

1 envelope plain gelatin
¼ cup cold water
½ cup hot water
1 tablespoon fresh lemon
    juice
1 teaspoon salt
Few drops onion juice

1 cup small-curd cottage
    cheese
1 medium-sized avocado,
    sieved
1 cup diced grapefruit
    sections

Soften gelatin in cold water and dissolve in hot water. Blend in lemon juice, salt, and onion juice. Cool. Force cottage cheese through sieve. Blend avocado and cheese into cooled gelatin. Fold in diced grapefruit sections. Turn into 6 individual molds. Chill until firm. Unmold.

Makes 6 servings.


## AVOCADO ORANGE MOLD

Serve this salad with Sunday's fried chicken.

1½ cups pear whole fruit
    nectar
2 tablespoons sugar
½ teaspoon salt
1 envelope plain gelatin

2 tablespoons cold water
¼ cup fresh lemon juice
1 large avocado, diced
½ cup finely chopped celery
⅔ cup orange sections

Heat nectar with sugar and salt. Soften gelatin in cold water and dissolve in hot nectar. Blend in lemon juice. Cool until slightly thickened. Fold avocado, celery, and orange into thickened gelatin. Pour into mold. Chill until firm. Unmold.

Makes 6 servings.

## AVOCADO STRAWBERRY MOLD

This is a salad with a wonderful velvety texture.

*1 envelope plain gelatin*
*¼ cup cold water*
*1 cup hot water*
*3 tablespoons fresh lemon*
*juice*
*1 tablespoon sugar*

*¾ teaspoon salt*
*1 medium-sized avocado,*
*sieved*
*1 cup halved fresh*
*strawberries*

Soften gelatin in cold water and dissolve in hot water. Stir in lemon juice, sugar, and salt. Cool. Stir avocado into cooled gelatin mixture. Fold in strawberries. Turn into mold. Chill until firm.
Makes 6 servings.

## AVOCADO VELVET ASPIC

Any celebration is an appropriate one for serving this aspic.

*1 3-ounce package lemon*
*gelatin*
*1 cup hot water*
*¾ cup cold water*
*2 tablespoons fresh lemon*
*juice*
*1 medium-sized avocado,*
*mashed*

*Dash salt*
*Dash Tabasco sauce*
*¼ cup mayonnaise*
*Pimiento strips*
*2 cups chilled grapefruit*
*sections*

Dissolve gelatin in hot water. Add cold water and lemon juice. Chill until slightly thickened. Dash mashed avocado with salt and Tabasco. Fold into gelatin along with mayonnaise. Blend until smooth. Lay strips of pimiento in bottom of mold. Fill with avocado aspic. Chill until firm. Unmold on garnished salad plate and circle with grapefruit sections.
Makes 6 servings.

## AVOCADO WINTER SALAD

Here is a salad that is a joy to serve and a joy to eat.

*1½ cups apricot whole fruit
   nectar*
*½ cup grapefruit juice*
*½ teaspoon salt*
*Few drops Tabasco sauce*
*1 tablespoon fresh lemon
   juice*

*1 teaspoon paprika*
*4 teaspoons plain gelatin*
*¼ cup cold water*
*¼ cup chopped sour pickle*
*3 medium-sized avocados*

Combine nectar, grapefruit juice, salt, Tabasco sauce, lemon juice, and paprika and heat to boiling. Remove from heat. Soften gelatin in cold water and dissolve in hot liquid. Stir in pickle. Divide equally among 6 molds. Chill until firm. Halve, seed, and peel avocados. Sprinkle halves inside and out with lemon juice and salt. Place each half on a garnished salad plate. Unmold gelatin onto centers of avocado halves.

Makes 6 servings.

## CALYPSO FRUIT MOLD

This salad mold has a distinctive foreign flavor.

*1 package lemon gelatin*
*1¾ cups hot water*
*2 tablespoons fresh lemon
   juice*
*Dash salt*
*1 medium-sized avocado,
   diced*

*1 cup orange sections*
*⅔ cup finely chopped
   celery*
*2 tablespoons chopped
   maraschino cherries*

Dissolve gelatin in hot water and blend in lemon juice and salt. Cool until slightly thickened. Fold avocado, orange, celery, and cherries into gelatin mixture. Turn into mold. Chill until firm. Unmold. Makes 6 servings.

## CHEESE SALAD MOLDS

A unique combination of cream cheese and avocado is in this salad.

1 envelope plain gelatin
2 tablespoons fresh lemon
  juice
1 8¼-ounce can sliced
  pineapple
½ teaspoon salt

1 teaspoon sugar
1 3-ounce package cream
  cheese
1 large avocado, sieved
¼ cup chopped nuts

Soften gelatin in lemon juice. Drain syrup from pineapple and add water to make 1 cup liquid. Heat with salt and sugar, and dissolve gelatin in it. Cool until mixture thickens slightly. Soften cheese with a fork and blend in cooled gelatin mixture, a tablespoon at a time. Stir in sieved avocado and nuts. Dice pineapple and add to gelatin mixture. Turn into individual molds. Chill until firm. Unmold.
Makes 6 servings.

## CITRUS SALAD MOLD

For a salad with a lovely cool color and an even better taste, serve this.

1 envelope plain gelatin
¼ cup cold water
1 cup hot water
½ cup fresh lemon juice
¾ teaspoon salt

1 medium-sized avocado,
  sieved
¾ cup diced orange sections
¾ cup diced grapefruit
  sections

Soften gelatin in cold water and dissolve in hot water. Blend in lemon juice and salt. Cool until slightly thickened. Blend avocado into gelatin. Fold in citrus fruits. Turn into mold. Chill until firm. Unmold.
Makes 6 servings.

## CREAMY AVOCADO SALAD

This extra special salad is worth the effort to make it.

*1 3-ounce package lemon
gelatin
1½ cups hot water
1½ cups diced grapefruit
sections
1 large avocado, sieved*

*2 3-ounce packages cream
cheese
1 envelope plain gelatin
2 tablespoons cold water
½ teaspoon celery salt
2 tablespoons cream*

Dissolve lemon gelatin in hot water. Cool. Stir in drained grapefruit and turn into large oiled mold. Chill. Combine sieved avocado with cheese and stir until smooth. Moisten plain gelatin in cold water and dissolve over hot water. Add slowly to avocado mixture, stirring continuously. Add celery salt and cream, and blend thoroughly. Spoon over firm grapefruit layer in mold. Chill until firm. To serve, unmold, slice, and arrange on garnished salad plates.
Makes 12 servings.

## ESCONDIDO SALAD

Smooth and exotic is this fruit salad.

*1 3-ounce package lemon
gelatin
1¾ cups hot water
2 tablespoons fresh lemon
juice
¼ teaspoon grated onion*

*Few grains salt
1 medium-sized grapefruit,
diced
1 medium-sized avocado,
diced*

Dissolve gelatin in hot water. Blend in lemon juice, onion, and salt. Cool until slightly thickened. Fold in diced grapefruit and avocado into gelatin. Turn into individual molds and chill until firm. Unmold.
Makes 6 servings.

## FIELD-FARE FRUIT SALAD

Prepare this lovely party salad for a June bride.

1 3-ounce package orange
  gelatin
1¾ cups hot water
¼ cup fresh lemon juice
1 medium-sized avocado,
  sliced

1 16-ounce can cling peach
  slices
1½ cups halved strawberries

Dissolve gelatin in hot water. Cool and stir in lemon juice. Cover bottom of 9-inch square pan with thin layer of gelatin. Arrange alternate slices of avocado and peaches in gelatin. Chill. Stir strawberries into remaining gelatin and pour over avocado and peach slices. Chill until firm. Unmold and serve upside down.
Makes 9 servings.

## FRUIT CHEESE MOLD

Here is a beautiful salad that combines avocado with ripe red strawberries.

1 envelope plain gelatin
¼ cup cold water
½ cup hot water
2 tablespoons fresh lemon
  juice
¾ teaspoon salt

1 cup small-curd cottage
  cheese
1 cup sliced fresh
  strawberries
Sugar
1 medium-sized avocado,
  cubed

Soften gelatin in cold water and dissolve in hot water. Add lemon juice and salt. Cool. Force cottage cheese through sieve and blend into gelatin mixture. Chill until slightly thickened. Slice strawberries and sprinkle lightly with sugar. Fold strawberries and avocado into slightly thickened gelatin mixture. Turn into mold and chill until firm. Unmold.
Makes 6 servings.

## FRUITED GUACAMOLE RING

This salad is welcome on Indian summer menus.

1½ tablespoons plain gelatin
¼ cup cold water
½ cup hot water
½ cup syrup from canned
   pineapple
¼ cup fresh lemon juice
1½ teaspoons salt

½ cup mayonnaise
2 large avocados, sieved
1 cup diced grapefruit
   sections
1 8¼-ounce can pineapple
   slices

Soften gelatin in cold water, and dissolve in hot water. Blend in pineapple syrup, lemon juice, and salt. Cool until slightly thickened. Fold mayonnaise, sieved avocados, and diced grapefruit sections into thickened gelatin. Cut drained pineapple slices in half and stand around side of mold. Carefully pour gelatin mixture into mold. Chill until firm. Unmold.
Makes 8 servings.

## GOLDEN RING SALAD

Here's a handsome salad you'll want to try during the Easter season.

2 3-ounce packages orange
   gelatin
2½ cups hot water
1 teaspoon grated orange rind
1½ cups orange juice

2 medium-sized avocados,
   cubed
Fresh lemon juice
Salt

Dissolve gelatin in hot water. Blend in orange rind and juice. Pour into 1-quart ring mold and chill until firm. Sprinkle cubed avocados with lemon juice and salt. Unmold gelatin onto garnished salad plate and fill center of ring with avocados.
Makes 8 servings.

## GRAPEFRUIT AVOCADO SALAD

Luncheon or dinner guests will approve of this unusual salad.

*1 envelope plain gelatin*
*¼ cup cold water*
*1 cup hot water*
*¼ cup fresh lemon juice*
*¼ cup sugar*
*½ teaspoon salt*

*1 3-ounce package cream*
*cheese*
*1 medium-sized avocado,*
*cubed*
*Salt*
*1 cup diced grapefruit*
*sections*

Soften gelatin in cold water and dissolve in hot water. Add 3 tablespoons lemon juice, sugar, and salt and mix well. Cool. To one half of this mixture add cream cheese softened with fork. Pour into bottom of small loaf pan. Chill until firm. Sprinkle cubed avocado with salt and remaining lemon juice. Add avocado and grapefruit to remaining gelatin mixture. Pour over cream cheese layer. Chill until firm. Unmold.

Makes 6 servings.

## GREEN 'N' GOLD SALAD

This is an expecially attractive salad for Thanksgiving.

*1½ tablespoons plain gelatin*
*¼ cup cold water*
*½ cup hot water*
*1 tablespoon sugar*
*¼ cup fresh lemon juice*

*1 teaspoon salt*
*1 medium-sized persimmon,*
*sieved*
*1 medium-sized avocado,*
*sieved*

Soften gelatin in cold water and dissolve in hot water. Blend in sugar, 3 tablespoons lemon juice, and ½ teaspoon salt. Cool. Add sieved persimmon to ½ cup of gelatin mixture. Pour into oiled loaf pan. Chill until almost firm. To remaining gelatin add sieved avocado, remaining lemon juice and salt. Mix well. Pour over firm persimmon layer. Chill until firm. Unmold.

Makes 6 servings.

## HAWAIIAN FRUIT MOLD

Here's a salad that will go well with a barbecue supper.

1 envelope plain gelatin
¼ cup fresh lemon juice
¼ cup sugar
½ teaspoon salt
1¼ cups hot water
¼ cup syrup from canned
 pineapple

1 medium-sized avocado,
 diced
1 cup finely shredded
 cabbage
¼ cup diced canned
 pineapple

Soften gelatin in lemon juice. Dissolve with sugar and salt in hot water. Blend in pineapple syrup and cool until slightly thickened. Fold diced avocado, cabbage and pineapple into thickened gelatin. Pour into oiled mold and chill until firm. Unmold. Makes 6 servings.

## HEAVENLY SALAD

Here's a simple salad that may well become a family favorite.

1 envelope plain gelatin
¾ cup cold water
¾ cup syrup from canned
 pineapple
¼ cup sugar
Dash salt
¼ cup fresh lemon juice

1 3-ounce package cream
 cheese
1 medium-sized avocado,
 cubed
1 cup canned pineapple
 chunks

Soften gelatin in ¼ cup cold water. Combine remaining ½ cup water with pineapple syrup, sugar, and salt. Heat. Dissolve softened gelatin in hot liquid. Blend in lemon juice. Cool until syrupy. Cut cream cheese into small cubes. Fold cheese cubes, avocado cubes, and pineapple chunks into gelatin. Turn into mold and chill until firm. Unmold.
Makes 6 servings.

## MIST GREEN SOUFFLÉ SALAD

A party-pretty salad like this one is often in demand.

*1 3-ounce package lime
gelatin
1 cup hot water
½ cup cold water
1 tablespoon fresh lemon
juice
½ cup mayonnaise*

*2 3-ounce packages cream
cheese
1 medium-sized avocado,
diced
1 medium-sized orange,
sliced*

Dissolve gelatin in hot water. Stir in cold water and lemon juice. Add mayonnaise and beat until smooth with rotary beater. Turn into refrigerator tray and place in freezing compartment 15 to 20 minutes, until mixture is set around edges and bottom of the tray. Turn gelatin mixture into bowl and beat with rotary beater until light and fluffy. Add softened cheese and beat again. Fold in fruit. Pour into mold and chill until firm. Unmold.
Makes 6 servings.

## PACIFIC ISLANDS MOLD

This colorful, tangy salad is for festive occasions.

*1 envelope plain gelatin
2 tablespoons cold water
1½ cups hot water
¼ cup sugar
¼ teaspoon salt
¼ cup fresh lemon juice*

*¼ teaspoon grated lemon
rind
1 large avocado, diced
⅔ cup halved canned
cherries
⅔ cup orange sections*

Soften gelatin in cold water and dissolve in hot water. Blend in sugar, salt, lemon juice and rind. Cool until slightly thickened. Fold fruit into thickened gelatin. Turn into mold and chill until firm. Unmold.
Makes 6 servings.

## RIO VISTA SALAD MOLDS

This is a delectable salad for extra special occasions.

2 3-ounce packages lemon
    gelatin
3 cups hot water
Few grains salt
1 8¼-ounce can undrained
    crushed pineapple

¼ cup fresh lemon juice
1 medium-sized avocado,
    sliced
2 3-ounce packages cream
    cheese
Table cream

Dissolve gelatin in hot water and blend in salt, pineapple, and lemon juice. Chill until slightly thickened. Add avocado slices very carefully to gelatin. Pour into molds and chill until firm. Unmold on garnished salad plates. Blend together cheese and sufficient cream to moisten; beat until fluffy. Use to top each serving.

Makes 8 servings.

## SANDRA'S FRUIT MOLDS

The fruits in this salad blend delightfully.

1 envelope plain gelatin
¼ cup cold water
1½ cups unsweetened
    grapefruit juice
¼ cup sugar

¼ teaspoon salt
2 medium-sized pears, diced
1 medium-sized avocado,
    diced
1 medium-sized banana, diced

Soften gelatin in water. Heat grapefruit juice, and dissolve softened gelatin, sugar, and salt in it. Cool until slightly thickened. Fold diced fruits into partially thickened gelatin. Turn into 6 individual molds, and chill until firm. Unmold.

Makes 6 servings.

## SAN JOSE LUNCHEON SALAD

Be prepared to grant requests for this recipe.

1 envelope plain gelatin
¼ cup cold water
½ cup hot water
1 teaspoon salt
1½ teaspoons grated onion
3 tablespoons fresh lemon
juice

Dash Tabasco sauce
1 cup small-curd cottage
cheese
1 medium-sized avocado,
sieved
Tart fresh fruit

Soften gelatin in cold water and dissolve in hot water. Stir in salt, onion, lemon juice, and Tabasco sauce. Cool until partially thickened. Mash cottage cheese through sieve. Add sieved avocado and cheese to thickened gelatin mixture. Mix well and turn into mold. Chill until firm. Serve with tart fresh fruit, such as grapefruit and orange sections.

Makes 6 servings.

## SIMPLICITY AVOCADO MOLD

Serve this simple salad with an elaborate dinner meal.

1 3-ounce package lime
gelatin
1¾ cups hot water

3 tablespoons fresh lemon
juice
2 medium-sized avocados,
diced

Dissolve gelatin in hot water. Stir in lemon juice. Chill until slightly thickened. Fold diced avocados into gelatin. Pour into 6 individual molds and chill until firm. Unmold.

Makes 6 servings.

## SPECIAL WALDORF SALAD

Try this medley of avocado, apple, and blanched almonds.

*1 3-ounce package lemon*
*gelatin*
*1½ cups hot water*
*1 teaspoon fresh lemon juice*
*¼ cup mayonnaise*
*1 tablespoon tomato catsup*
*¼ teaspoon prepared mustard*

*1 medium-sized avocado,*
*diced*
*½ cup finely chopped celery*
*1 cup diced apple*
*½ cup slivered blanched*
*almonds*

Dissolve gelatin in hot water. Blend in lemon juice. Cool. Combine mayonnaise, catsup, and mustard and blend with gelatin. Chill until slightly thickened. Fold avocado, celery, apple, and almonds into thickened gelatin. Turn into shallow pan or individual molds. Chill until firm. Unmold. Makes 6 servings.

## SUMMER GLITTER RING

An avocado and cantaloupe salad provides an original combination.

*2 3-ounce packages lime*
*gelatin*
*2¼ cups hot water*
*½ cup fresh lemon juice*
*8 to 10 fresh mint leaves*

*1 cup chilled ginger ale*
*1 medium-sized cantaloupe*
*1 medium-sized avocado*
*1 17-ounce can fruit cocktail*

Dissolve gelatin in hot water. Add lemon juice, whole mint leaves. Cool, discard mint, then add ginger ale. Chill until slightly thickened. Cut 4 or 5 slices of cantaloupe for top of mold. Dice the rest. Cut 4 or 5 slices of avocado for decoration. Dice the rest. Arrange cantaloupe and avocado slices in bottom of ring mold in pattern. Set with a thin film of gelatin. Add diced fruit and drained fruit cocktail to gelatin. Spoon into mold. Chill until firm. Unmold. Makes 10 servings.

## TAIWAN FRUIT MOLD

Pears and ginger combined with avocados have a new and unique flavor.

*1 3-ounce package lime gelatin*
*1¾ cups hot water*
*¼ cup lemon juice*
*1 large avocado, diced*

*1 cup diced fresh or canned pears*
*2 tablespoons finely chopped preserved ginger*

Dissolve gelatin in hot water. Blend in lemon juice and cool until slightly thickened. Fold avocado, pears, and ginger into thickened gelatin. Pour into mold and chill until firm. Unmold.
Makes 6 servings.

## TEMPTING FRUIT MOLD

Pamper your family and serve this tempting fruit mold.

*½ cup syrup from canned pineapple*
*½ cup water*
*1 3-ounce package lime gelatin*
*2 tablespoons fresh lemon juice*
*1½ cups small-curd cottage cheese*

*3 tablespoons diced pimiento*
*3 tablespoons diced green pepper*
*1 cup diced canned pineapple*
*1 medium-sized avocado, diced*

Combine pineapple syrup and water, and heat to boiling. Dissolve gelatin in it. Blend in lemon juice, and cool to room temperature. Force cottage cheese through a sieve. Stir gelatin into cheese gradually, blending well. Stir pimiento, green pepper, pineapple, and avocado into gelatin mixture. Turn into mold and chill until firm. Unmold.
Makes 8 servings.

## THERESA'S BUFFET SALAD

Avocado blends especially well with grapefruit and orange.

2 3-ounce packages lemon
 gelatin
3½ cups hot water
Few drops Tabasco sauce
1 teaspoon prepared
 horseradish

6 tablespoons lemon juice
2 medium-sized avocados,
 sliced
Salt
Grapefruit sections
Orange sections

Dissolve gelatin in hot water and blend in Tabasco sauce, horse-radish, and 3 tablespoons lemon juice. Chill until slightly thickened. Sprinkle avocado slices with remaining lemon juice and salt. Cover bottom of mold with gelatin and chill until thick. Add a layer of avocado slices. Finish filling mold with alternate layers of gelatin and avocado slices, using gelatin for top layer. Chill until firm. Unmold and fill center with grapefruit and orange sections.

Makes 10 servings.

## Molded Meat Salads

### DELECTABLE SHERRY-VEAL MOLD

For a gourmet meal serve this.

2 pounds veal shank
1 medium-sized onion, peeled
2 medium-sized carrots,
 peeled
1 envelope plain gelatin
2 teaspoons cold water

2¼ cups broth from veal
¼ teaspoon onion salt
Salt
2 teaspoons sherry
2 large avocados, diced
¾ cup chopped sweet pickles

Cover veal with cold, salted water. Add onion and cook slowly until meat is tender (about 2½ to 3 hours). Add carrots for last 30 to 40 minutes. When meat is tender, lift from liquid. Strain liquid and measure and, if necessary, boil down to required amount. Dice carrots and veal and discard onion. Moisten gelatin in cold water. Combine gelatin, broth, onion salt, salt to taste, and wine. Chill until broth starts to congeal. Add diced avocados, veal, carrots, and pickles, and blend lightly. Pour into oiled mold and chill overnight.

Makes 8 servings.

## HAM-AVOCADO MOUSSE

Have this at a patio party.

| | |
|---|---|
| 1 10½-ounce can chicken broth or consommé | ¾ cup ground ham |
| 1 egg yolk | 1 egg white |
| 1 envelope plain gelatin | ½ cup whipping cream |
| 2 medium-sized avocados | Radish roses, if desired |
| 1 tablespoon fresh lemon juice | Ripe olives |
| | Lime or lemon wedges |

Heat ⅔ cup of the chicken broth. Add slightly beaten egg yolk and cook, stirring, until thickened. Soften gelatin in remaining chicken broth. Add to hot broth and stir until dissolved. Chill until syrupy. Put 1½ avocados through sieve with lemon juice and a little of gelatin mixture to make blending easier. Add ham and remaining gelatin. Beat egg white until stiff; then with the same beater, whip cream. Fold avocado mixture into cream, then fold in egg white. Pour into mold. Chill until firm. Unmold and fill center with radish roses (if desired) and ripe olives. Garnish with lime or lemon wedges and slices of remaining avocado.

Makes 8 servings.

## HAM SUPPER SALAD

Now is the time to try out this salad for a Sunday-night supper.

*1 envelope plain gelatin*
*2 tablespoons lemon juice*
*1 tablespoon vinegar*
*1⅓ cups hot water*
*1½ teaspoons salt*
*1 teaspoon grated onion*
*⅓ cup mayonnaise*
*1 teaspoon prepared mustard*

*1 medium-sized avocado,*
*diced*
*1 cup diced cooked ham*
*2 hard-cooked eggs, diced*
*1 cup shredded cabbage*
*2 tablespoons chopped dill*
*pickle*

Soften gelatin in lemon juice and vinegar, and dissolve in hot water. Blend in salt and onion. Cool until slightly thickened. Blend in mayonnaise and mustard. Fold avocado, ham, eggs, cabbage, and pickle into gelatin. Turn into mold. Chill until firm. Unmold. Makes 6 servings.

## *Molded Poultry Salads*

## CHICKEN ASPIC SUPREME

Here's a chicken and avocado salad for a festive buffet supper.

*1½ cups chicken broth*
*½ teaspoon celery salt*
*1 envelope plain gelatin*
*¼ cup cold water*
*½ cup ripe olives*
*1 large avocado, cubed*

*2 tablespoons minced sour*
*pickle*
*2 teaspoons fresh lemon juice*
*2 canned pimientos, sliced*
*1 cup minced cooked*
*chicken*

Heat broth and celery salt to boiling. Soften gelatin in cold water and dissolve in hot broth. Cool until slightly thickened. Cut olives into large pieces. Fold avocado, olives, pickle, lemon juice, pimiento, and chicken into thickened gelatin. Turn into mold and chill until firm. Unmold. Makes 6 to 8 servings.

## CHICKEN SALAD ROYAL

For a meal that gives you distinction as a hostess, serve this.

1 envelope plain gelatin
2 tablespoons fresh lemon
  juice
2 chicken bouillon cubes
½ teaspoon salt
1¾ cups hot water

⅓ cup mayonnaise
1 medium-sized avocado,
  diced
1 cup diced cooked chicken
¾ cup diced apple

Soften gelatin in lemon juice and dissolve with bouillon cubes and salt in hot water. Cool until slightly thickened. Stir in mayonnaise. Fold avocado, chicken, and apple into gelatin. Turn into mold and chill until firm. Unmold.

Makes 6 servings.

## SAN MARCOS AVOCADO LOAF

Serve this whole-meal salad some hot summer day.

1 medium-sized avocado,
  cubed
1½ cups diced cooked
  chicken
½ cup chopped green pepper
½ cup finely chopped celery
3 tablespoons fresh lemon
  juice

3¼ cups hot water
3 chicken bouillon cubes
½ teaspoon celery salt
2½ tablespoons plain gelatin
½ cup cold water
¼ cup mayonnaise

Combine avocado with chicken, pepper, celery, and lemon juice. Pour hot water over chicken bouillon cubes and celery salt. Soften gelatin in cold water and dissolve in hot bouillon. Chill until slightly thickened. Add mayonnaise to avocado mixture, blending lightly. Add to bouillon mixture. Pour into oiled mold and chill until firm. Unmold.

Makes 6 to 8 servings.

## Molded Seafood Salads—Fish

### AVOCADO BOUNTIFUL SALAD

If you've had a busy day, prepare this meal-in-one salad.

| | |
|---|---|
| 1 3-ounce package lemon gelatin | ¾ cup flaked prepared seafood |
| 1½ cups hot water | 8 thick slices peeled tomato |
| 1 large avocado, cubed | Lettuce |
| ½ cup finely chopped celery | Salt |
| ⅔ cup finely chopped carrot | |
| 4 tablespoons fresh lemon juice | |

Dissolve gelatin in hot water and chill until slightly thickened. Combine avocado with celery, carrot, lemon juice, and seafood. Blend into thickened gelatin. Pour into pan and chill until firm. Place one slice of tomato on each lettuce-garnished salad plate and sprinkle with salt. Top with squares of avocado gelatin. Makes 8 servings.

### AVOCADO ENTREE SALAD

Serve this salad at a luncheon honoring special guests.

| | |
|---|---|
| 1 10½-ounce can consommé | ⅔ cup flaked prepared seafood |
| Few drops Tabasco sauce | 3 medium-sized avocados |
| 1 envelope plain gelatin | Lemon juice |
| 2 tablespoons cold water | Salt |
| 1 teaspoon minced onion | |

Combine soup and Tabasco sauce and heat to boiling. Soften gelatin in cold water and dissolve in hot soup. Chill to consistency of unbeaten egg white. Blend in onion and seafood. Chill until firm. Halve, seed, and peel avocados. Sprinkle with lemon juice and salt. Place one avocado half on each garnished salad plate and fill with consommé cubes.

Makes 6 servings.

## BUENA VISTA SALAD

Here's a rich, creamy, and delectable salad.

2 envelopes plain gelatin
1 tablespoon cold water
⅓ cup French dressing
½ cup whipping cream
⅔ cup mayonnaise
1 teaspoon fresh lemon juice

3 tablespoons pickle relish
1 cup flaked prepared
seafood
1 large avocado, cubed
1 canned pimiento, chopped

Soften gelatin in cold water. Heat French dressing and dissolve softened gelatin in it. Cool. Whip cream and fold in mayonnaise; then blend in French dressing mixture. Add lemon juice, pickle relish, seafood, and avocado. Pour into flat mold or pan. Sprinkle chopped pimiento over top. Chill until firm. Cut into squares and serve on garnished plates.

Makes 6 to 8 servings.

## CARMEL SALAD MOLD

Tuna and crisp cabbage are good partners with avocado.

1 envelope plain gelatin
¼ cup fresh lemon juice
1 tablespoon sugar
1½ teaspoons salt
1¼ cups hot water
1 tablespoon grated onion

1 medium-sized avocado,
sieved
¾ cup flaked cooked or
canned tuna
¾ cup finely shredded
cabbage

Soften gelatin in lemon juice. Dissolve sugar, salt, and softened gelatin in hot water. Blend in onion. Cool. Blend avocado into cooked gelatin and chill until slightly thickened. Fold in tuna and cabbage, and turn into loaf pan. Chill until firm. Unmold.

Makes 6 servings.

*Gail's Chiffonade Salad.* This salad combination of chicken and avocado is an example of creative cuisine. (page 105)

## FRANCISCAN TUNA LOAF

Keep last-minute preparations to a minimum by serving a tuna loaf salad.

1 medium-sized avocado,
  cubed
1½ cups flaked canned tuna
½ cup grated carrot
½ cup finely chopped celery
3 tablespoons fresh lemon
  juice

2 envelopes plain gelatin
½ cup cold water
3 chicken bouillon cubes
½ teaspoon salt
3 cups hot water
¼ cup mayonnaise

Combine cubed avocado with tuna, carrot, celery, and lemon juice. Soften gelatin in cold water. Dissolve bouillon cubes, salt, and softened gelatin in hot water. Chill until slightly thickened. Blend in mayonnaise and avocado mixture. Pour into loaf pan and chill until firm. Unmold.

Makes 6 to 8 servings.

## FRESNO SALMON SALAD

Try salmon in a tart mold with mellow avocado.

1 envelope plain gelatin
1¼ cups water
1 10½-ounce can consommé
1 tablespoon fresh lemon
  juice
¼ cup mayonnaise

1 cup canned or cooked
  salmon
1 medium-sized avocado,
  diced
Salt
¾ cup finely chopped celery
¼ cup diced green pepper

Soften gelatin in ¼ cup cold water. Heat remaining water and dissolve gelatin in it. Stir in consommé and lemon juice. Cool until slightly thickened. Blend mayonnaise into ¼ cup of gelatin mixture, and divide among 8 individual molds. Chill until set, while preparing remaining ingredients. Drain and flake salmon coarsely. Sprinkle avocado lightly with salt. Fold salmon, avocado, celery and green pepper into remaining gelatin. Spoon carefully over mayonnaise layer in molds. Chill until firm. Unmold.

Makes 8 servings.

## HARVEST MOON SALAD LOAF

Impromptu entertaining is easy with this salad loaf.

*1 envelope plain gelatin*
*¼ cup cold water*
*½ cup hot water*
*2 tablespoons fresh lemon juice*
*1 teaspoon salt*
*1 tablespoon grated onion*
*Dash Tabasco sauce*

*1½ cups small-curd cottage cheese*
*1 large avocado, diced*
*3 tablespoons chopped pimiento*
*¾ cup finely chopped celery*
*¾ cup flaked sardines*

Soften gelatin in cold water and dissolve in hot water. Blend in lemon juice, salt, onion, and Tabasco. Cool. Force cheese through sieve and blend into gelatin mixture. Fold diced avocado, pimiento, celery, and fish into gelatin mixture. Turn into loaf pan and chill until firm. Cut into slices to serve.

Makes 6 servings.

## SOUTHWEST SALMON LOAF

Treat your guests to this handsome luncheon salad.

*1 envelope plain gelatin*
*¼ cup fresh lemon juice*
*2 chicken bouillon cubes*
*½ teaspoon salt*
*1¼ cups hot water*
*½ teaspoon curry powder*

*1 tablespoon grated onion*
*2 cups canned or cooked salmon*
*1 medium-sized avocado, diced*
*½ cup finely chopped celery*

Soften gelatin in lemon juice. Dissolve softened gelatin, bouillon cubes and salt in hot water. Blend in curry powder and onion. Cool until slightly thickened. Flake salmon. Fold avocado, salmon, and celery into thickened gelatin mixture. Turn into loaf pan and chill until firm. Unmold. Slice to serve.

Makes 6 servings.

## TWO-LAYER ELEGANT SALAD

For a modern look, try this company salad.

TUNA LAYER:

| | |
|---|---|
| 1 envelope plain gelatin | ½ teaspoon salt |
| ¼ cup cold water | ¼ cup mayonnaise |
| 1 cup hot water | 1 cup finely chopped celery |
| 2 tablespoons fresh lemon juice | 1 cup flaked tuna |
| | ¼ cup diced pimiento |

AVOCADO LAYER:

| | |
|---|---|
| 1 envelope plain gelatin | 1 teaspoon salt |
| ¼ cup cold water | 1 large avocado, sieved |
| ⅔ cup hot water | ½ cup dairy sour cream |
| 2 teaspoons fresh lemon juice | Dash Tabasco sauce |

*Tuna Layer:* Soften gelatin in cold water and dissolve in hot water. Blend in lemon juice and salt. Cool to consistency of unbeaten egg white. Fold in mayonnaise, celery, tuna, and pimiento. Divide among individual molds and chill while preparing second layer.

*Avocado Layer:* Soften gelatin in cold water and dissolve in hot water. Blend in lemon juice and salt. Cool to room temperature. Blend avocado, sour cream, and Tabasco sauce into cooled gelatin. Spoon into molds over tuna layer and chill until firm. Unmold.

Makes 8 servings.

## SPRING SALMON SALAD

Here's a salmon salad that deserves a place in the salad parade.

1 envelope plain gelatin
2 tablespoons fresh lemon
  juice
1 cup hot water
1¼ teaspoons salt
2 teaspoons grated onion
1 medium-sized avocado,
  sieved

½ cup mayonnaise
1 cup flaked, cooked or
  canned salmon
½ cup chopped cucumber
1 cup finely sliced cooked
  asparagus

Soften gelatin in lemon juice and dissolve in hot water. Blend
in salt and onion. Cool until slightly thickened. Blend avocado and
mayonnaise into gelatin. Stir in salmon, cucumber, and asparagus.
Turn into individual molds and chill until firm.
Makes 6 servings.


## TUNA SALAD SELECT

Everyone likes tuna for luncheon, especially with avocados.

1 envelope plain gelatin
¼ cup fresh lemon juice
3 tablespoons sugar
1 teaspoon salt
1¼ cups hot water
¼ cup vinegar from sweet
  pickles

1 medium-sized avocado,
  diced
1 cup grated tuna
¾ cup finely chopped celery
¼ cup sliced sweet pickles

Soften gelatin in lemon juice. Dissolve softened gelatin, sugar,
and salt in hot water. Add vinegar from pickles. Cool until
slightly thickened. Fold avocado, tuna, celery, and pickles into
thickened gelatin. Turn into loaf pan and chill until firm. Unmold.
Makes 6 servings.

## Molded Seafood Salads—Shrimp

### JEAN'S SHRIMP RING

Prepare a very appetizing salad for spring meals.

2 3-ounce packages lime
    gelatin
2 cups hot water
1½ cups cold water
5 tablespoons fresh lemon
    juice

Tabasco sauce to taste
2 medium-sized avocados,
    sliced
1½ cups prepared shrimp

Dissolve gelatin in hot water and stir in cold water, lemon juice and Tabasco sauce. Chill until slightly thickened. Add sliced avocados and shrimp cut into halves to thickened gelatin, mixing lightly. Pour into 9-inch ring mold and chill until firm. Unmold. Makes 8 servings.

### PIEDMONT SHRIMP SQUARES

Add this recipe to your collection of shrimp favorites.

1 3-ounce package lime
    gelatin
1½ cups hot water
1 large avocado, cubed
¾ cup finely diced cucumber
½ cup sliced ripe olives

5 tablespoons fresh lemon
    juice
Onion salt
¾ cup halved prepared
    shrimp
Sliced tomatoes

Dissolve gelatin in hot water. Chill until slightly thickened. Combine avocado with cucumber, olives, lemon juice, a dash of onion salt, and shrimp. Stir into chilled gelatin and blend lightly. Turn into oiled mold and chill until firm. Cut into squares and serve on sliced tomatoes.
Makes 8 servings.

## PINK SHRIMP MOLDS

This is a gelatin salad that saves you from last-minute preparations.

1 envelope plain gelatin
2 tablespoons fresh lemon
  juice
1⅓ cups hot water
½ teaspoon salt
½ teaspoon grated onion
¼ cup chili sauce
⅓ cup mayonnaise

1 medium-sized avocado,
  diced
1¼ cups cleaned cooked
  shrimp
2 hard-cooked eggs, diced
¾ cup finely chopped celery
2 tablespoons chopped green
  pepper

Soften gelatin in lemon juice and dissolve in hot water. Blend in salt, onion, and chili sauce. Cool until slightly thickened. Blend in mayonnaise. Fold avocado, shrimp, eggs, celery, and green pepper into gelatin mixture. Turn into individual molds and chill until firm. Unmold.
Makes 8 servings.

## PIXIE SHRIMP MOLDS

Here's a salad pretty enough to serve as a dinner masterpiece.

2 cups puréed cooked
  tomatoes
½ teaspoon celery salt
Few drops Tabasco sauce
4 teaspoons plain gelatin
2 tablespoons cold water

1 medium-sized avocado,
  diced
1 tablespoon fresh lemon
  juice
1 cup prepared shrimp

Combine tomatoes, celery salt, and Tabasco sauce, and heat to boiling. Soften gelatin in cold water and dissolve in hot mixture. Chill until slightly thickened. Sprinkle diced avocado with lemon juice. Stir avocado and shrimp into thickened gelatin. Pour into individual molds. Chill until firm. Unmold.
Makes 6 servings.

## Molded Vegetable Salads

### AFTERGLOW SALAD

Watch faces brighten when you serve this.

*1 envelope plain gelatin*
*¼ cup cold water*
*1 vegetable bouillon cube*
*1½ cups hot water*
*¼ cup finely chopped green pepper*

*2 hard-cooked eggs, diced*
*¼ cup finely chopped celery*
*½ cup mayonnaise*
*1 small avocado, cubed*

Soften gelatin in cold water. Dissolve softened gelatin and bouillon cube in hot water. Cool until slightly thickened. Stir in pepper, eggs, celery, and mayonnaise. Fold avocado into cooled gelatin mixture. Turn into mold and chill until firm. Unmold and slice. Makes 6 servings.

### AVOCADO ASPIC MOLD WITH VEGETABLES

You will win praise with this original salad.

*2 envelopes plain gelatin*
*½ cup cold water*
*3 cups hot chicken broth*
*¼ cup fresh lemon juice*
*½ teaspoon salt*

*2 large avocados, diced*
*2 tablespoons diced pimiento*
*1 package frozen mixed vegetables*
*French dressing*

Soften gelatin in cold water and dissolve in hot chicken broth. Blend in lemon juice and salt. Cool until slightly thickened. Fold in avocados and pimiento. Spoon into 9-inch ring mold. Chill until firm. Meanwhile, cook frozen vegetables according to package directions. Drain. Mix lightly with French dressing, and chill thoroughly. Turn ring mold out onto serving dish, fill center with vegetables.
Makes 6 to 8 servings.

## AVOCADO CHEESE MOLDS

Treat the family to a salad to satisfy hungry appetites.

| | |
|---|---|
| *1 envelope plain gelatin* | *Dash Tabasco sauce* |
| *2 tablespoons cold water* | *1 teaspoon vinegar* |
| *1¾ cups hot tomato juice* | *1 medium avocado, diced* |
| *½ teaspoon salt* | *¼ pound shredded processed* |
| *½ teaspoon grated onion* | *cheese* |
| *Few drops Worcestershire* | *¾ cup finely chopped celery* |
| *sauce* | |

Soften gelatin in cold water and dissolve in hot tomato juice. Blend in salt, onion, Worcestershire sauce, Tabasco sauce, and vinegar. Cool until slightly thickened. Fold avocado, cheese, and celery into slightly thickened gelatin. Turn into individual molds and chill until firm. Unmold.

Makes 6 to 8 servings.

## AVOCADO DINNER SALAD ASPIC

Use this salad as a surprise for your guests.

| | |
|---|---|
| *1 cup hot water* | *½ cup mayonnaise* |
| *2 chicken bouillon cubes* | *1 large avocado, cubed* |
| *1 envelope plain gelatin* | *½ cup chopped ripe olives* |
| *2 tablespoons cold water* | *3 tablespoons pickle relish* |

Pour hot water over bouillon cubes. Soften gelatin in cold water and dissolve in hot bouillon. Cool slightly and stir in mayonnaise. Fold cubed avocado, olives, and pickle relish into thickened gelatin mixture. Turn into mold and chill until firm. Unmold.

Makes 6 servings.

## AVOCADO MEJICANO SALAD

Colorful and flavorful is this salad.

1 envelope plain gelatin
3 tablespoons cold water
1 cup hot water
1 large avocado, sieved
3 tablespoons fresh lemon
   juice

¼ teaspoon salt
1 teaspoon grated onion
2 tablespoons chopped
   pimiento

Soften gelatin in cold water and dissolve in hot water. Chill until slightly thickened. Blend together sieved avocado, lemon juice, salt, onion, and pimiento. Stir mixture into thickened gelatin. Pour into shallow pan and chill until firm. Unmold and cut into squares.
Makes 4 servings.

## AVOCADO VEGETABLE SALAD MOLDS

Gourmets who welcome a new flavor experience will enjoy this salad.

1 envelope plain gelatin
¼ cup cold water
1½ cups hot tomato juice
½ teaspoon salt
2 tablespoons vinegar

1 medium-sized avocado,
   diced
1 12-ounce can mixed
   vegetables
1 tablespoon instant minced
   onion

Soften gelatin in cold water and dissolve in hot tomato juice. Blend in salt and vinegar. Cool until slightly thickened. Fold avocado, drained vegetables, and onion into gelatin. Turn into molds and chill until firm. Unmold.
Makes 6 servings.

## AVOCADO VEGETABLE SURPRISE

If you want a salad that is distinctive in both appearance and flavor, try this vegetable salad.

*1 envelope plain gelatin*
*½ cup cold water*
*1 cup hot water*
*¼ cup sugar*
*1 teaspoon salt*
*2 tablespoons vinegar*
*2 tablespoons fresh lemon*
  *juice*

*2 tablespoons grated onion*
*1 medium-sized avocado,*
  *cubed*
*½ cup finely chopped celery*
*½ cup chopped cooked or*
  *canned beets*

Soften gelatin in cold water and dissolve in hot water. Stir in sugar, salt, vinegar, lemon juice, and onion. Cool until slightly thickened. Fold avocado, celery, and beets into gelatin mixture. Pour into mold. Chill until firm. Unmold.
Makes 6 servings.

## BELVEDERE SALAD MOLDS

Here's a salad you will serve frequently.

*1 envelope plain gelatin*
*2 tablespoons cold water*
*½ cup boiling water*
*1¼ teaspoons salt*
*2 tablespoons vinegar*
*1 tablespoon fresh lemon*
  *juice*
*2 tablespoons grated raw*
  *onion*

*1 medium-sized avocado,*
  *sieved*
*⅓ cup dairy sour cream*
*¾ cup finely chopped celery*
*¼ cup chopped green pepper*
*2 tablespoons chopped*
  *pimiento*

Soften gelatin in cold water and dissolve in boiling water. Blend in salt, vinegar, lemon juice, and onion. Cool. Blend avocado and

sour cream into cooled gelatin mixture. Fold in celery, pepper, and pimiento. Turn into individual molds. Chill until firm. Unmold.
Makes 5 to 6 servings.

## CONFETTI SALAD MOLDS

Serve this tantalizing salad with a dinner casserole.

| | |
|---|---|
| 1 3-ounce package lime gelatin | 1 large avocado, cubed |
| 1⅔ cups hot water | ¼ cup chopped green pepper |
| 4 tablespoons vinegar | ¼ cup diced pimiento |
| ¼ teaspoon salt | 1 cup finely chopped celery |

Dissolve gelatin in hot water. Blend in vinegar and salt. Cool until slightly thickened. Fold avocado, green pepper, pimiento, and celery into gelatin. Turn into individual molds and chill until firm. Unmold.
Makes 6 servings.

## EUGENIA'S SPRING SALAD

This salad is as promising as spring.

| | |
|---|---|
| 1 3-ounce package lemon gelatin | Salt |
| | ½ cup finely chopped celery |
| 1¾ cups hot water | ½ cup grated carrot |
| 1 large avocado, diced | 2 tablespoons chopped green |
| 2 tablespoons fresh lemon juice | pepper |

Dissolve gelatin in hot water. Chill until thick but not firm, whip until light and frothy. Sprinkle avocado with lemon juice and salt. Add avocado, celery, carrot, and green pepper to whipped gelatin, blending lightly. Pour into loaf pan and chill until firm. Unmold.
Makes 6 servings.

## GARDEN SALAD MOLD

A summer barbecue would be the ideal time for a salad mold such as this.

1 3-ounce package lemon
   gelatin
1¾ cups hot water
2 tablespoons fresh lemon
   juice

¾ cup finely diced cucumber
⅓ cup sweet pickle relish
Few drops Tabasco sauce
1 medium-sized avocado,
   diced

Dissolve gelatin in hot water and stir in lemon juice. Chill until slightly thickened. Stir cucumber, pickle relish, Tabasco sauce, and avocado into gelatin. Pour into mold and chill until firm. Unmold. Makes 4 servings.


## MANDARIN SALAD

An elegant salad does wonders to dress up a family meal.

1 envelope plain gelatin
2 tablespoons fresh lemon
   juice
¾ cup boiling water
1 teaspoon salt
1 teaspoon grated onion

Dash Tabasco sauce
1 large avocado, sieved
½ cup chilled evaporated
   milk
¼ cup diced pimiento
¼ cup diced green pepper

Soften gelatin in lemon juice, and dissolve in boiling water. Blend in salt, onion, and Tabasco sauce. Cool to room temperature. Blend sieved avocado into cooled gelatin. Whip evaporated milk in chilled bowl until light and fluffy. Fold into avocado mixture. Fold in pimiento and pepper. Turn into mold and chill until firm. Unmold.
Makes 5 to 6 servings.

## NEWPORT AVOCADO SALAD

Here's a party salad that will please.

1 envelope plain gelatin
3 tablespoons fresh lemon
   juice
1 cup hot water
2 teaspoons salt
1 teaspoon sugar

Dash Tabasco sauce
1 large avocado, sieved
⅓ cup mayonnaise
3 cups finely shredded
   cabbage
¼ cup chopped pimiento

Soften gelatin in lemon juice and dissolve in hot water. Blend in salt, sugar, and Tabasco sauce. Cool until slightly thickened. Blend in avocado and mayonnaise with gelatin. Fold in cabbage and pimiento. Turn into mold and chill until firm. Unmold.
Makes 6 to 8 servings.

## SAN BERNARDINO BUFFET SALAD

You can count on praise for this flavorsome salad.

1½ tablespoons plain gelatin
¼ cup cold water
2½ cups cooked or canned
   tomatoes
1 bay leaf
5 whole cloves

¼ cup minced onion
½ teaspoon salt
Dash pepper
Dash Tabasco sauce
1 large avocado, diced
½ cup finely chopped celery

Soften gelatin in cold water. Combine tomatoes, bay leaf, cloves, onion, salt, pepper, and Tabasco sauce, and boil together 5 minutes. Strain. Dissolve softened gelatin in hot liquid and chill until slightly thickened. Fold diced avocado and celery into thickened gelatin. Turn into mold. Chill until firm. Unmold.
Makes 6 servings.

## SOUR CREAM AVOCADO MOLDS

Leftover turkey and these sour-cream molds seem to go together.

1 envelope plain gelatin
2 tablespoons cold water
½ cup boiling water
1¼ teaspoons salt
2 tablespoons vinegar
1 tablespoon lemon juice
2 tablespoons minced onion

1 medium-sized avocado,
    sieved
⅓ cup dairy sour cream
¾ cup finely chopped celery
¼ chopped green pepper
2 tablespoons chopped
    pimiento

Soften gelatin in cold water and dissolve in boiling water. Blend in salt, vinegar, lemon juice, and onion. Cool. Blend avocado and sour cream into cooled gelatin mixture. Fold in celery, pepper, and pimiento. Turn into individual molds and chill until firm. Unmold.
Makes 5 to 6 servings.

## TANGY AVOCADO MOLD

Give zest to your winter meals and prepare a most unusual salad.

1 envelope plain gelatin
⅓ cup cold water
2 medium-sized avocados,
    sieved
2⅓ cups buttermilk

½ cup mayonnaise
1½ teaspoons salt
2 tablespoons grated onion
Dash Tabasco sauce

Soften gelatin in cold water and dissolve by setting over hot water. Cool slightly. Add sieved avocados. Stir together buttermilk, mayonnaise, salt, onion, and Tabasco sauce. Gradually mix in gelatin. Turn into mold and chill until firm. Unmold.
Makes 8 servings.

# UNMOLDED SALADS

A simply arranged or tossed salad with an appropriate dressing is a wise choice for a first course at dinner. Among the absolutely necessary requirements for unmolded salads are freshness of ingredients, appetizing flavor, pleasing color combinations, an excellent salad dressing, and all ingredients must be very cold. The use of avocados transforms even the simplest salad into one that is *extraordinaire*. So—paint your salads green, with avocados, of course.

## *Unmolded Fruit Salads*

### ANGEL ISLAND SALAD

Here's a minty salad that is good winter or summer.

| | |
|---|---|
| 1 17-ounce can cling peach slices | Fresh lemon juice |
| 1 to 2 drops mint extract | Salt |
| 1 medium-sized avocado, sliced | 1 large grapefruit, sectioned |

Combine undrained peaches with mint extract, cover and let stand an hour or more. Sprinkle avocado with lemon juice and salt. Drain peaches. Arrange avocado slices, grapefruit sections, and peach slices on crisp salad greens.

Makes 4 servings.

## AUTUMN JUBILEE SALAD

Serve this luncheon salad with great expectations.

| | |
|---|---|
| *1 medium-sized avocado,* | *2 medium-sized grapefruit* |
| *diced* | *1 dozen green ripe olives* |
| *Salt* | |

Sprinkle avocado with salt. Cut grapefruit into halves crosswise and remove fruit in segments, cutting off all white membrane, and leaving shells whole. Clip out any remaining membrane from shells. Combine diced avocado and grapefruit segments, sprinkle lightly with salt and pile into grapefruit shells. Cut olives into wedges and arrange over salad.
Makes 4 servings.

## AVOCADO-APPLE HALVES

For a different Waldorf salad with mellow avocado, serve this.

| | |
|---|---|
| *2 medium-sized red-skinned* | *⅓ cup chopped celery* |
| *apples* | *½ cup mayonnaise* |
| *¼ cup raisins* | *½ teaspoon salt* |
| *¼ cup chopped nuts* | *3 medium-sized avocados* |

Core and dice apples. Add remaining ingredients except avocados. Toss lightly. Halve, seed, and peel avocados. Fill with apple salad mixture.
Makes 6 servings.

## AVOCADO CANTALOUPE PLATE

Add interest to a meal with an avocado-cantaloupe combination.

| | |
|---|---|
| *2 medium-sized avocados,* | *Lemon juice* |
| *sliced* | *1 medium-sized cantaloupe* |
| *Salt* | |

Sprinkle avocados with salt and lemon juice. Cut cantaloupe into thin lengthwise slices and remove skin. Arrange alternate slices of avocado and melon in a fan pattern on crisp salad greens.

Makes 4 to 6 servings.

## AVOCADO FRUIT RINGS

Present guests with a flavorsome salad that is so easy to prepare.

| | |
|---|---|
| 1 large avocado | Salt to taste |
| 1 20½-ounce can pineapple | Dash Tabasco sauce |
| spears | Lemon juice |
| ½ cup dairy sour cream | |

Cut unpeeled avocado in halves crosswise. Remove seed. Cut slices from each half. Peel each ring individually. Put 2 to 3 pineapple spears through center of each ring. Mash remaining avocado and mix with sour cream, salt, and Tabasco sauce. Add lemon juice to taste.

Makes 6 to 8 servings.

## AVOCADO LUCKY SALAD

Use this salad when you wish to serve one that is especially attractive.

| | |
|---|---|
| 1 large orange, sectioned | Salt |
| 2 medium-sized avocados | 1 cup cottage cheese |
| Lemon juice | 2 maraschino cherries, halved |

Chill orange sections. Halve, seed, and peel avocados. Sprinkle with lemon juice and salt. Place one half on each garnished plate. Fill center with mound of cottage cheese. Top with orange sections and cherry halves.

Makes 4 servings.

## AVOCADO MARVEL SALAD

This salad helps to make your dinner a delight.

3 medium-sized avocados,        ¾ cup shredded coconut
    sliced                          ¾ cup mayonnaise
3 medium-sized oranges,         3 tablespoons orange juice
    sectioned                       3 tablespoons sugar

Put avocados, oranges, and coconut in a bowl. Combine mayonnaise, orange juice, and sugar. Pour over fruit and coconut and toss lightly.
Makes 8 servings.


## AVOCADO PARTY SALAD

A salad studded with fruit is always a favorite.

2 medium-sized avocados
Salt
1¾ cups chilled, cubed, mixed fruit

Halve, seed, and peel avocados. Sprinkle with salt. Fill halves with mixed fruit. Makes 4 servings.


## AVOCADO-PINEAPPLE SALAD

Here is a luscious salad everyone will like.

1 small avocado, diced          ¼ teaspoon salt
1 medium-sized tomato, diced    4 cups mixed salad greens
½ cup fresh pineapple, cubed    French dressing
1 tablespoon minced onion

Combine all salad ingredients and toss lightly with French dressing. Makes 4 servings.

## FASCINATION SALAD

To suit the occasion or make one, serve this salad.

1 19-ounce can sliced peaches
1 medium-sized avocado,
  sliced
Fresh lemon juice

Salt
1 medium-sized grapefruit,
  sectioned
French dressing

Drain peaches thoroughly. Sprinkle avocado with lemon juice and salt. Alternate peach slices, grapefruit sections, and avocado slices on garnished plates. Serve with French dressing.
Makes 4 servings.

## GRANADA SALAD BOWL

Treat the family to this salad anytime.

6 cups crisp salad greens
2 medium-sized oranges,
  diced
2 green onions, sliced
¼ cup salad oil
1½ tablespoons fresh lemon
  juice

½ teaspoon salt
¼ teaspoon mustard
¼ teaspoon paprika
¼ teaspoon pepper
1 medium-sized avocado,
  diced

Break greens into bite-sized pieces in large salad bowl. Add oranges and onions to greens. Combine next six ingredients in small jar and shake thoroughly to blend. Drizzle over salad mixture and toss lightly until all greens are coated. Add avocado and toss again lightly. Serve at once.
Makes 6 servings.

## JAPANESE FAN SALAD

Lovely to look at and lovely to eat is this salad.

2 medium-sized avocados,
sliced
Fresh lemon juice
Salt

2 medium-sized oranges,
sliced
French dressing

Sprinkle avocados with lemon juice and salt. Arrange avocado slices fan shape on garnished salad plates. Place orange slices in semicircle to form top of fan. Serve with French dressing.
Makes 4 servings.


## JIFFY AVOCADO SALAD

This is an easy and festive way to start a company meal.

1 17-ounce can fruit cocktail
2 medium-sized avocados,
sliced

Fresh lemon juice
Salt
French dressing

Chill fruit cocktail thoroughly and drain. Sprinkle avocado slices with lemon juice and salt. Arrange avocado slices on salad greens and top with fruit cocktail. Serve with French dressing.
Makes 4 servings.


## LAZY SUSAN SALAD

This salad is a charmer for that special luncheon.

3 medium-sized avocados
Fresh lemon juice
2 medium-sized grapefruit,
sectioned

6 tiny whole cooked beets
Blue cheese dressing

Halve and seed avocados. Sprinkle with lemon juice. Arrange grapefruit sections and beets in avocado halves. Serve with blue cheese dressing.

Makes 6 servings.

## LOVELY NUT SALAD

For those who like nuts and avocados this is just right.

3 medium-sized avocados,
  sliced
Lemon juice
1 20½-ounce can pineapple
  slices

½ pint whipping cream
2 tablespoons sugar
½ cup chopped pecans

Sprinkle avocados with lemon juice. Alternate avocado and pineapple on garnished salad plate. Whip cream with sugar until stiff. Fold in nuts. Spoon over avocado and pineapple.

Makes 8 servings.

## MAUI FRUIT PLATE

This salad will steal the show at party affairs.

1 medium-sized avocado,
  sliced
Fresh lemon juice
Salt
1 8¼-ounce can sliced
  pineapple

2 cups shredded lettuce
Mayonnaise
Orange sections
Cream cheese balls

Sprinkle avocado with lemon juice and salt. Arrange pineapple around edge of garnished serving plate. Place two avocado slices on each pineapple slice. Cut remaining avocado into small pieces and combine with shredded lettuce. Toss lightly with mayonnaise thinned with a bit of lemon juice. Pile in center of plate. Garnish with orange sections and cream cheese balls.

Makes 4 servings.

## MINTED FRUIT SALAD

A refreshing mint sauce enhances avocado and fruits.

1 15¼-ounce can pineapple
   tidbits
1 teaspoon plain gelatin
¼ cup cold water
1 tablespoon sugar
Pinch salt
1 tablespoon lemon juice

¼ teaspoon mint extract
1 medium-sized red apple,
   diced
⅓ cup sliced fresh or canned
   peaches
½ cup finely chopped celery
3 medium-sized avocados

Drain pineapple, reserving syrup. Soften gelatin in cold water. Heat pineapple syrup to a boil. Add gelatin with sugar and salt. Stir to dissolve. Add lemon juice and mint extract. Chill until slightly thickened. Combine pineapple, apple, peaches and celery. Halve, seed, and peel avocados. Spoon fruit mixture into half-shells on garnished salad plates. Drizzle with minted gelatin.

Makes 6 servings.

## NOVEL FRUIT SALAD

When in doubt, try this popular salad.

3 medium-sized avocados
1 8¼-ounce can crushed
   pineapple

2 tablespoons chopped green
   pepper
1 cup cottage cheese
French dressing

Halve, seed, and peel avocados. Arrange avocados on garnished salad plates. Combine pineapple, green pepper, and cottage cheese. Mix lightly. Spoon cottage cheese mixture into avocado half-shells. Serve with French dressing.

Makes 6 servings.

## PEACH AVOCADO SURPRISE

For a novel salad, prepare this.

1 19-ounce can cling peach
    slices
3 cups shredded cabbage
3 tablespoons chopped pecans
1 teaspoon salt

½ cup dairy sour cream
2 tablespoons lemon juice
2 tablespoons sugar
3 medium-sized avocados

Drain peaches. Combine peaches, cabbage, and pecans. Mix salt, sour cream, lemon juice, and sugar. Pour over cabbage mixture and toss lightly. Chill. Halve and seed avocados. Spoon cabbage mixture into avocado half-shells.

Makes 6 servings.

## SAN JOAQUIN SALAD

A conversation will start with this salad.

2 medium-sized avocados
Salt
Fresh lemon juice
⅓ cup ripe olives

2 medium-sized grapefruit,
    sectioned
French dressing

Halve and seed avocados. Scoop out part of fruit, leaving a thin layer in shell. Cut scooped-out portion into cubes and sprinkle with salt and lemon juice. Cut olives into pieces. Combine with cubed avocado and sectioned grapefruit and toss together lightly. Place in avocado shells. Top with French dressing and chill.

Makes 4 servings.

## SOUTH SEAS AVOCADO SALAD

Almost any man will enjoy this salad.

2 medium-sized avocados  
Fresh lemon juice  
Salt  
2 medium-sized oranges,  
    sectioned  
½ cup mayonnaise

½ teaspoon prepared mustard  
2 teaspoons tomato catsup  
¼ cup finely chopped celery  
1 teaspoon prepared  
    horseradish

Halve and seed avocados. Sprinkle fruit with lemon juice and salt. Starting at seed cavity, remove 3 small wedges of avocado at equal intervals on both sides of each half-shell, like a scalloped edge. Insert one section of orange in avocado where each wedge has been removed. Dice wedges of avocado and combine with mayonnaise, mustard, catsup, celery, horseradish, and remaining orange sections. Blend thoroughly. Place in center of avocado half-shells. Serve on garnished salad plates.

Makes 4 servings.

## TRADE WINDS SALAD

This is a salad that will please sophisticates.

1 small clove garlic  
2 medium-sized oranges,  
    sectioned  
French dressing

1 medium-sized avocado  
1 tablespoon crumbled  
    Roquefort cheese

Rub inside of small bowl with cut clove of garlic. Place oranges in bowl and cover with French dressing. Let stand while preparing

*Ham-Avocado Mousse* is a conversation piece as well as a joy to eat. (page 70)

*San Marcos Avocado Loaf,* garnished with avocado rings "threaded" with pineapple spears, is superb. (page 72)

9

*Avocado Aspic Mold with Vegetables* is made with a chicken broth base. Cubes of avocado and diced pimiento give wonderful flavor and color. Fill the mold with the chilled, cooked vegetables. (page 81)

remainder of salad. Cut avocado into quarters lengthwise, seed and peel. Place 1 quarter on each garnished salad plate. Fill with orange sections and sprinkle with Roquefort cheese.

Makes 4 servings.

## TROPHY SALAD

Here's a salad easy to make and very handsome.

| | |
|---|---|
| 1 medium-sized avocado, sieved | Salt |
| 2 teaspoons lemon juice | 2 medium-sized oranges, sectioned |
| 1 cup cottage cheese | |

Add lemon juice to sieved avocado. Fold in cottage cheese and mix together lightly. Season with salt. Chill. Pile spoonfuls of mixture on garnished salad plate. Top with orange sections.

Makes 4 to 6 servings.

## VAGABOND FRUIT SALAD

If you want a salad to go with almost any meal, here is a good choice.

| | |
|---|---|
| 2 medium-sized avocados | 1 cup cubed fresh pear |
| Lemon juice | 1 cup halved orange sections |
| Salt | |

Halve and seed avocados. Sprinkle with lemon juice and salt. Place half-shells on garnished salad plates. Combine pear and orange and place in half-shells.

Makes 4 servings.

## ZIPPY SALAD BOWL

If you serve this salad you will have an attractive color accent.

| | |
|---|---|
| 1 medium-sized grapefruit, sectioned | Salt |
| 4 cups torn lettuce | Pepper |
| 1 small carrot, shredded | 3 tablespoons salad oil |
| 1 medium-sized avocado, diced | |

Squeeze into bowl any grapefruit juice which remains in membranes. Cut each grapefruit section into halves in bowl. Add lettuce, carrot, and avocado. Sprinkle with salt and pepper. Add oil and toss lightly to blend.

Makes 5 to 6 servings.

## *Unmolded Meat Salads*

## ALAMEDA CHEF'S SALAD

Dinner guests will always remember this salad.

| | |
|---|---|
| 1 large grapefruit, sectioned | ¼ teaspoon paprika |
| ¼ cup salad oil | Pepper |
| 1 tablespoon fresh lemon juice | 6 cups broken salad greens |
| 1 teaspoon salt | 1 large tomato |
| ¼ teaspoon dry mustard | 4 thin slices ham |
| ¼ teaspoon celery seed | 1 large avocado, sliced |
| | Green pepper strips |

Prepare grapefruit, working over a bowl to catch juice. Combine grapefruit juice with salad oil, lemon juice, salt, mustard, celery seed, paprika and pepper to taste. Mix well by shaking together in small jar. Pour about ¾ of dressing over salad greens and toss lightly. Cut tomato into sixths. Cut ham into thin slivers. Arrange grapefruit sections, avocado slices, tomato wedges and ham slivers in 6 groups around top of bowl of salad greens. Garnish with green pepper strips. Drizzle remaining dressing over top of bowl. Serve at once.

Makes 6 servings.

## BRAVADO SALAD

A perfect barbecue partner is this salad.

| | |
|---|---|
| 1 cup dairy sour cream | 3 cups cubed cooked |
| 1½ teaspoons salt | potatoes |
| ½ teaspoon seasoned pepper | ¼ cup minced onion |
| ½ teaspoon caraway seed | 8 slices cooked bacon, |
| 2 tablespoons lemon juice | crumbled |
| 3 medium-sized avocados | 1 large tomato |
| ¼ cup chopped parsley | |

Blend sour cream with salt, pepper, caraway seed, and 1 tablespoon lemon juice. Cut 2 avocados into cubes. Combine with chopped parsley, potatoes, onion, cream mixture, and half of bacon in salad bowl. Toss lightly. Arrange ring of parsley sprigs around outside edge. Cover with foil or plastic wrap. Chill. Just before serving, core tomato and slice crosswise. Cut slices into halves. Cut remaining avocado into slices and sprinkle with lemon juice. Arrange tomato and avocado slices alternately on top of salad. Sprinkle remaining bacon into center.

Makes 6 to 8 servings.

## CLUB SALAD BOWL

Serve this in summer for a main salad for supper.

| | |
|---|---|
| 1 large avocado, cubed | French dressing |
| 1 cup finely chopped celery | 8 to 10 cooked or canned |
| 1 cup diced cooked ham or | asparagus spears |
| pressed ham | 1 hard-cooked egg, sliced |
| 2 tablespoons sliced green | |
| onion | |

Combine avocado, celery, ham, and onion, and toss lightly with French dressing. Place in garnished bowl. Top with asparagus spears and hard-cooked egg.

Makes 6 servings.

## GOLDEN STATE SALAD

With very little effort, here is a main dish salad you can serve.

| | |
|---|---|
| 6 cups torn salad greens | ½ cucumber, diced |
| 2 green onions, thinly sliced | 1 large tomato, sliced |
| 6 radishes, thinly sliced | 4 hard-cooked eggs, sliced |
| 1 medium-sized avocado, | 4 slices bologna or luncheon |
| cubed | meat |
| Fresh lemon juice | 4 slices cheese |
| Salt | French dressing |

Place salad greens, onions, and radishes in large bowl. Sprinkle avocado with lemon juice and salt. On top of lettuce place avocado, cucumber, tomato, and eggs. Cut meat and cheese into thin strips and add. Pour the French dressing over the salad. Toss lightly. Serve at once.

Makes 4 servings.

## SHEFFIELD SALAD

Looking for a distinctive salad for distinctive people? Here's one.

2 medium-sized avocados, sliced
Lemon juice
1 12-ounce can pork luncheon meat

2 large tomatoes
1 large onion
Lettuce
Ripe olives

Sprinkle avocado slices with lemon juice. Cut meat into 12 slices. Slice tomatoes. Cut onion into rings. Line four salad plates with lettuce. Arrange 4 or 5 slices avocado, 3 slices meat, 2 slices tomato and several onion rings on each plate. Garnish with olives. Makes 4 servings.

## SUMMER TOSSED SALAD

Serve this substantial salad for the main course.

6 cups crisp salad greens
1 cup diced cooked ham
½ cup diced pineapple
1 large avocado, diced
1 thinly sliced green onion

¼ cup salad oil
1½ tablespoons vinegar
1 teaspoon salt
⅛ teaspoon dry mustard
⅛ teaspoon pepper

Combine greens, ham, pineapple, avocado, and onion in salad bowl. Blend oil, vinegar, salt, mustard, and pepper, and pour over salad mixture. Toss very lightly until all of greens are coated with dressing. Serve at once.
Makes 6 servings.

## TREASURE ISLAND SALAD

For a different filled avocado and tomato salad serve this.

18 double Saltine crackers,        ½ cup salad dressing
    crumbled                      1 4½-ounce can deviled ham
½ onion, minced                    2 medium-sized avocados
¼ teaspoon pepper                  4 medium-sized tomatoes
2 hard-cooked eggs, chopped

In large bowl blend together cracker crumbs, onion, pepper, and chopped eggs. In another bowl mix salad dressing and deviled ham. Blend salad dressing mixture into crumb mixture and toss. Halve and seed avocados. Remove centers from tomatoes. Stuff mixture into avocados and tomatoes. Serve on garnished platter.
Makes 8 servings.


## *Unmolded Poultry Salads*


## BEVERLY HILLS CHICKEN SALAD

Leftover chicken is the main ingredient here.

2 medium-sized avocados       1 cup cooked chicken pieces
Fresh lemon juice             ¼ teaspoon dry mustard
Salt                          Mayonnaise
1 cup finely chopped celery   Jellied cranberry sauce

Halve, seed, and peel avocados. Sprinkle with lemon juice and salt. Arrange on salad plates. Combine celery, chicken, and mustard and mix with sufficient mayonnaise to moisten. Top avocado halves with chicken mixture. Garnish with balls cut from cranberry sauce.
Makes 4 servings.

## GAIL'S CHIFFONADE SALAD

When you serve this salad the rest of the menu is easy.

2 cups diced cooked chicken
1 cup finely chopped celery
2 teaspoons grated lemon
   peel
1½ tablespoons lemon juice
1 green onion, chopped
½ teaspoon salt

¼ teaspoon paprika
½ cup white wine or
   grapefruit juice
1 avocado, diced
½ cup slivered almonds
⅓ cup mayonnaise

Combine chicken, celery, lemon peel and juice, onion, salt, paprika, and wine or grapefruit juice. Chill 2 to 3 hours. When ready to serve add avocado, almonds, and mayonnaise to chicken mixture. Toss lightly.
Makes 4 servings.

## HOLIDAY TURKEY SALAD

Begin or end the holiday season with this salad.

SALAD:

1 large avocado
Fresh lemon juice
Salt
1 cup finely chopped celery

1½ cups diced cooked turkey
Cream Dressing
Jellied cranberry sauce

CREAM DRESSING:

2 tablespoons salad oil
1 tablespoon flour
¼ teaspoon salt
3 tablespoons sugar
1 teaspoon prepared mustard

1 teaspoon paprika
⅓ cup cider vinegar
⅓ cup water
2 eggs, beaten
¼ cup whipping cream

Halve, seed, peel, and quarter avocado. Sprinkle with lemon juice and salt. Lightly mix celery and turkey with enough Cream Dressing to moisten. Arrange avocado quarters on garnished salad plates and fill centers with turkey and celery. Top with slices of cranberry sauce. Serve additional dressing, if desired.

*Cream Dressing:* Rub salad oil and flour to a paste. Combine salt, sugar, mustard, paprika, vinegar, and water; bring to a boil. Pour over paste and blend well. Add to beaten eggs and stir briskly to avoid curdling. Return to heat and bring to boiling point but do not boil. Remove from heat and stir in cream. Cool.

Makes 4 servings.

## Unmolded Seafood Salads—Crab

### COMPANY ALASKA SALAD

Serve a crab salad for your next dinner party or buffet.

2 medium-sized avocados
2 tablespoons lemon juice
¼ teaspoon wine vinegar
½ teaspoons salt
¼ cup salad oil
¼ cup mayonnaise

2 cups crab meat
1½ cups finely chopped celery
2 tablespoons minced green onion

Sieve or mash 1 avocado. With rotary beater, beat in lemon juice, vinegar, salt. Gradually beat in salad oil, then mayonnaise. Peel, seed, and cube second avocado and add to crab meat, celery, and onion. Toss with part of the dressing. Chill. Mound salad on 4 garnished plates. Top with rest of dressing.

Makes 4 servings.

## CORONA DEL MAR CRAB

Here is a salad that provides extraordinary eating satisfaction.

2 cups flaked crab meat
1 cup finely chopped celery
½ cup mayonnaise
¼ cup chili sauce
Lemon juice

Salt
3 medium-sized avocados
8 slices crisp bacon, crumbled
2 hard-cooked eggs, sliced

Toss together the crab meat, celery, mayonnaise, chili sauce, and 1 tablespoon lemon juice. Add salt to taste. Chill. Halve, seed, and peel avocados and sprinkle with lemon juice. Place on garnished plates. Add bacon to crab mixture; toss lightly and mound into avocado halves. Garnish with slices of egg.

Makes 6 servings.

## LAKE TAHOE CLUB SALAD

If it's a salad with mealtime goodness you wish, here is the one.

1 medium-sized avocado
Fresh lemon juice
Salt
1½ cups flaked crab meat
½ cup mayonnaise
½ cup finely chopped celery

¼ cup chopped red radishes
  (optional)
2 tablespoons lemon juice
Dash Tabasco sauce
Few drops Worcestershire
  sauce

Seed, peel, and quarter avocado. Sprinkle with lemon juice and salt. Arrange on garnished salad plates; top with crab meat. Combine mayonnaise with remaining ingredients; spoon over crab.

Makes 4 servings.

## Unmolded Seafood Salads—Fish

### ALEUTIAN ISLANDS SALMON SALAD

Salmon and avocado make an ideal taste combination.

1½ cups cooked or canned
  salmon
1 large avocado, diced
1½ cups finely chopped
  celery

2 cups mayonnaise
2 tablespoons lemon juice
3 tablespoons pickle relish

Remove bones and flake salmon. Add avocado and celery. Blend mayonnaise, lemon juice, and pickle relish. Blend lightly with salmon. Serve on garnished salad plates.
Makes 6 servings.

### ARTISTE TUNA SALAD

Tuna lovers will like this salad.

1 medium-sized avocado,
  cubed
2 tablespoons lemon juice
¼ teaspoon salt
1 6½-ounce can tuna,
  drained and flaked
¾ cup mayonnaise

¼ cup seafood cocktail sauce
½ tablespoon prepared
  mustard
3 tablespoons finely chopped
  green pepper
Corn chips

Sprinkle avocado with lemon juice and salt. Combine with tuna. Spoon into garnished salad bowls. Combine mayonnaise, cocktail sauce, mustard, and green pepper. Spoon over avocado and tuna mixture. Sprinkle with lightly crushed corn chips.
Makes 6 servings.

## COLUMBIA RIVER SALMON SALAD

This is a delightful salad for a winter luncheon.

| | |
|---|---|
| 2 medium-sized avocados | 1 cup flaked canned or |
| Fresh lemon juice | cooked salmon |
| Salt | ⅓ cup sliced ripe olives |
| ⅓ cup finely chopped celery | French dressing |

Halve, seed, and peel avocados. Sprinkle with lemon juice and salt. Combine celery, salmon, and olives, and marinate in French dressing. Place avocado halves on garnished salad plates and fill with salmon mixture.

Makes 4 servings.

## GOURMET HALF-SHELLS

Make this salad and listen to the compliments.

| | |
|---|---|
| 3 medium-sized avocados | 2 tablespoons finely chopped |
| Fresh lemon juice | parsley |
| Salt | 2 teaspoons chopped chives |
| 1 cup finely chopped celery | Mayonnaise |
| 1 cup flaked seafood | |
| 2 tablespoons minced sour | |
| pickle | |

Halve, seed, and peel avocados. Sprinkle with lemon juice and salt. Combine celery, seafood, pickle, parsley, chives, and salt to taste, with sufficient mayonnaise to moisten. Toss together lightly. Place an avocado half-shell on each of 6 garnished salad plates. Fill with seafood mixture.

Makes 6 servings.

## LYNN'S TUNA LUNCHEON SALAD

The chances are you'll please everybody with this.

| | |
|---|---|
| *1 large avocado* | *1 6½-ounce can chunk-style* |
| *Fresh lemon juice* | *tuna, flaked* |
| *Salt* | *½ cup mayonnaise* |
| *1 green pepper* | *¼ teaspoon salt* |
| *2 cups finely chopped celery* | *Dash Tabasco sauce* |
| | *Paprika* |

Cut avocado into halves crosswise and seed. Cut each half into 3 rings. Remove skin and sprinkle with lemon juice and salt. Cut pepper into 6 rings and remove seeds. Arrange avocado and pepper rings on garnished salad plate. Combine celery, fish, mayonnaise, salt, 1 teaspoon lemon juice, and Tabasco sauce; blend well. Heap onto pepper and avocado rings. Sprinkle with paprika.
    Makes 6 servings.

## PUGET SOUND SALMON SALAD

To add special color to a salad, use salmon.

*1 8-ounce can red salmon*
*2 large tomatoes*
*1 medium-sized avocado, cubed*
*1 small head lettuce*

Drain and flake salmon. Dice tomatoes. Combine avocado, tomato, and salmon. Remove outer leaves of lettuce and save for garnish. Break remaining lettuce into bite-sized pieces. Serve on lettuce.
    Makes 4 to 6 servings.

## TOSSED TUNA SALAD

When appetites are listless, serve this tossed tuna salad.

*8 cups coarsely shredded
lettuce*
*2 green onions*
*1 6½-ounce can chunk-style
tuna*

*1 medium-sized tomato, diced*
*1 medium-sized avocado,
diced*
*Salt and pepper*
*French dressing*

Shred or break lettuce into salad bowl. Slice onions thinly. Drain oil from tuna. Flake tuna over top. Add tomato and avocado. Sprinkle with salt and pepper to taste. Toss lightly with French dressing. Serve at once.
Makes 6 servings.

## TUNA SALAD ARISTOCRAT

Discriminating luncheon guests will certainly enjoy this salad.

*3 medium-sized avocados*
*Fresh lemon juice*
*Salt*
*1 6½-ounce can chunk-style
tuna*

*1½ cups shredded lettuce*
*6 tablespoons mayonnaise*
*3 tablespoons tomato catsup*
*1 teaspoon prepared mustard*

Halve and seed avocados. Sprinkle with lemon juice and salt. Combine tuna and lettuce. Blend together mayonnaise, catsup, and mustard. Pour over tuna and lettuce, and toss together lightly. Fill half-shells with tuna mixture and serve on garnished salad plates.
Makes 6 servings.

## VENETIAN INTRIGUE

You can usually count on people appreciating a salad such as this.

2 *medium-sized avocados*  
*Fresh lemon juice*  
*Salt*  
1 *medium-sized tomato,*  
*cubed*

⅔ *cup flaked cooked lobster*  
⅓ *cup finely chopped celery*  
2 *tablespoons mayonnaise*  
*French dressing*

Halve and seed avocados. Sprinkle with lemon juice and salt. Combine tomato, lobster, celery, mayonnaise, and salt to taste. Mix lightly and spoon into avocado half-shells. Arrange on garnished salad plate. Serve with French dressing.
Makes 4 servings.

## *Unmolded Seafood Salads—Shrimp*

### HEARTY SPRING SALAD

Here is a hearty salad to be enjoyed by all partakers.

1 *large avocado*  
2 *large tomatoes*  
8 *to* 12 *cooked asparagus*  
*spears*  
1 *cup cleaned cooked shrimp*  
1 *cup finely chopped celery*

2 *hard-cooked eggs, diced*  
⅓ *cup mayonnaise*  
1 *tablespoon fresh lemon*  
*juice*  
*Salt*  
*Pepper*

Halve, seed, and peel avocado. Cut into crosswise slices. Peel and slice tomatoes. Arrange tomatoes, avocado slices, and asparagus on garnished salad plates. Combine shrimp, celery, and egg. Blend mayonnaise and lemon juice and mix lightly with shrimp mixture. Season to taste with salt and pepper. Serve over tomato, avocado, and asparagus.

Makes 4 to 6 servings.

## SHRIMP SAGA SALAD

This is outstanding as a first-course salad.

| | |
|---|---|
| 1 clove garlic | 2 tablespoons chopped |
| ⅓ cup salad oil | pimiento |
| 2 tablespoons tarragon wine | Salad greens |
| vinegar | 1 medium onion |
| ½ teaspoon salt | 2 large tomatoes |
| Pepper | 1 7-ounce can shrimp |
| Dash Tabasco sauce | 1 medium-sized avocado, |
| 2 tablespoons chopped | sliced |
| canned green chilies | |

Peel and crush garlic. Combine with oil, vinegar, and seasonings in a jar. Cover and shake vigorously. Add chilies and pimiento. Fill bowl with bite-sized salad greens. Peel and slice onion and quarter tomatoes. Add to greens along with cleaned, drained seafood. Combine avocado with other ingredients. Pour dressing over salad and toss lightly.

Makes 6 servings.

## SHRIMP SALAD TRIUMPH

Almost anyone will enjoy this salad, brimful of tasty goodness.

| | |
|---|---|
| 2 medium-sized avocados | 1¼ cups cleaned cooked |
| Fresh lemon juice | shrimp |
| Salt | French dressing |
| 2 canned pimientos | |

Halve and seed avocados. Sprinkle with lemon juice and salt. Dice pimientos and combine with shrimp. Place avocado halves on garnished salad plates and fill with shrimp mixture. Serve with French dressing.

Makes 4 servings.

## STUFFED TOMATOES, BOLINAS STYLE

You can usually count on people appreciating a salad such as this.

| | |
|---|---|
| 1 medium-sized avocado | ½ cup finely chopped celery |
| 4 teaspoons lemon juice | ½ cup chopped ripe olives |
| 2 teaspoons minced onion | ¾ cup diced cooked shrimp |
| Salt | French dressing |
| 6 chilled medium-sized tomatoes | |

Mash avocado. Blend in lemon juice, onion, and salt to taste. Peel tomatoes. Cut a slice from top and hollow out each tomato. Dice pulp. Sprinkle inside of tomato shells with salt. Combine diced tomato, celery, olives, shrimp, and French dressing. Blend lightly. Place tomato shells on garnished salad plates and fill with shrimp mixture. Cover tops generously with prepared avocado.

Makes 6 servings.

## TROPICAL COURT SALAD

Invite guests to share this delectable salad.

| | |
|---|---|
| 1 medium-sized avocado, sliced | 1½ cups cleaned cooked shrimp |
| Fresh lemon juice | ¼ cup sliced green onion |
| Salt | ½ cup mayonnaise |
| 1 small head lettuce | Lemon wedges |
| French dressing | |

Sprinkle avocado with lemon juice and salt. Cut lettuce into four thick slices. Place on salad plates and sprinkle with French dressing. Combine shrimp, onion, and mayonnaise and heap on top of each lettuce slice. Cover with avocado slices. Garnish each salad with a lemon wedge.

Makes 4 servings.

## Unmolded Vegetable Salads

### ACACIA SALAD

Fit this salad into your Easter menu.

1 large avocado, sliced
Fresh lemon juice
Salt
1 pint cottage cheese
⅓ cup finely chopped sweet
    pickle

¼ cup chopped green pepper
1 hard-cooked egg
French dressing

Sprinkle avocado with lemon juice and salt. Combine cheese, pickle, salt to taste, and green pepper. Place a mound of cheese mixture on garnished salad plates and arrange avocado slices, petal fashion, around cheese. Force hard-cooked egg through a sieve and sprinkle over cheese. Serve with French dressing.

Makes 6 servings.

### ANTIPASTO SALAD

Here you have a salad that takes only minutes to prepare.

1 large avocado, cubed
1 cup cooked red kidney
    beans
½ cup sliced green onion

1 cup shredded lettuce
⅛ teaspoon dried orégano
French dressing

Combine avocado with beans, onion, and lettuce. Sprinkle with orégano. Toss lightly with French dressing. Arrange on garnished salad plates.

Makes 4 to 6 servings.

## AVOCADO ROQUEFORT SALAD

This salad can easily be enlarged for a buffet.

*1 large avocado*
*Fresh lemon juice*
*Salt*
*2 medium-sized tomatoes,*
    *peeled*

*¼ cup sieved Roquefort*
    *cheese*
*6 tablespoons mayonnaise*

Halve, seed, and peel avocado. Cut crosswise into medium-thin rings. Sprinkle with lemon juice and salt. Cut tomatoes into wedges. Blend together cheese and mayonnaise. Arrange avocado rings and tomato wedges on garnished plate. Top with cheese mixture.

Makes 4 servings.

## AVOCADO TOPMOST

This versatile salad is good for family or company menus.

*1 10½-ounce can condensed*
    *consommé*
*3 medium-sized avocados*
*Fresh lemon juice*
*Salt*

*⅓ cup minced green onion*
    *or chives*
*⅓ cup finely chopped celery*
*Dairy sour cream*

Chill soup overnight in can. Halve and seed avocados. Sprinkle with lemon juice and salt. Place avocado half-shells on garnished salad plates and fill with jellied consommé. Sprinkle with onion or chives, and celery. Top with sour cream. Serve at once.

Makes 6 servings.

## AVOCADO VINAIGRETTE

For an appetite-teaser, serve this.

SALAD:

1 large avocado
1 medium-sized tomato
1 hard-cooked egg, chopped
Lettuce

DRESSING:

¼ cup salad oil
1½ tablespoons wine vinegar
1 tablespoon chopped parsley
1 tablespoon chopped chives
1 tablespoon chopped green
  pepper

¼ teaspoon salt
Dash pepper
1 tablespoon chopped
  pimiento

*Salad:* Cut avocado into quarters and remove seed and skin. On each garnished salad plate arrange a tomato slice with an avocado quarter cut into slices. Pour dressing over salad and sprinkle with egg.

*Dressing:* Combine all ingredients for dressing in small jar and shake well to blend just before serving.

Makes 4 servings.

## BARBARA'S BEET SALAD

This salad is pretty enough for a Sunday dinner.

2 tablespoons sugar
½ teaspoon salt
Dash cloves
¼ cup lemon juice
¼ cup beet liquid

1½ cups sliced cooked beets
1 medium-sized avocado
Salt
French dressing

Combine sugar, salt, cloves, ¼ cup lemon juice and beet liquid. Stir until sugar is dissolved. Pour over beets and let stand 2 hours or longer. Just before serving, halve, seed, and peel avocado. Cut into lengthwise wedges and sprinkle with salt. Arrange drained beets and avocado wedges on garnished plate. Serve with French dressing.

Makes 4 servings.

## CORNUCOPIA SALAD

This salad should rate high with guests and family.

½ cup ripe olives
⅔ cup finely chopped celery
⅔ cup diced tomato
¼ cup sliced sweet pickle
2 medium-sized avocados

Salt
Fresh lemon juice
¼ cup French dressing
1 tablespoon catsup

Cut olives into large pieces. Blend celery, tomato, olives, and pickle. Halve, seed, and peel avocados. Sprinkle cut surfaces with salt and lemon juice. Arrange each half-shell on garnished salad plate and fill with vegetable mixture. Serve with French dressing blended with catsup.

Makes 4 servings.

## CRISPY CABBAGE IN AVOCADO RINGS

Cabbage and avocado make this a very different kind of salad.

1 large avocado
Lemon juice
Salt
2 cups shredded crisp
   cabbage

½ cup diced cucumber
1 teaspoon minced onion
1 pimento, chopped
French dressing

Cut avocado crosswise into halves and remove seed. Cut two rings from each half and remove skin. Sprinkle with lemon juice and salt. Place 1 ring on each of 4 garnished salad plates.

Combine cabbage, cucumber, onion, pimiento, and diced end pieces of avocado with French dressing. Toss together lightly. Pile in center of avocado rings.

Makes 4 servings.

## FESTIVE POTATO SALAD

Don't let summer go by before you serve this.

1 clove garlic
1 large avocado, cubed
2 cups diced cold boiled
   potato
1 cup finely chopped celery

¼ cup sliced green onion
¼ cup chopped sweet pickle
1 teaspoon salt
1 cup mayonnaise
2 teaspoons lemon juice

Rub mixing bowl lightly with cut clove of garlic. Combine avocado, potato, celery, onion, and pickle. Sprinkle with salt. Add mayonnaise and lemon juice, and blend lightly. Chill. Arrange on serving platter.

Makes 6 to 8 servings.

## GOOD LUCK SALAD BOWL

What is better than a salad, crisp and fresh?

2 hard-cooked eggs
¼ cup oil
1 tablespoon sugar
1½ tablespoons vinegar
2 tablespoons water
1½ teaspoons salt

Dash pepper
¼ teaspoon celery seed
6 cups bite-sized pieces
   lettuce
1 medium-sized avocado,
   diced

Mash yolks of eggs and blend in oil, sugar, vinegar, water, salt, pepper, and celery seed. Place lettuce in large bowl. Chop egg white and sprinkle over lettuce. Add avocado. Pour oil-vinegar mixture over all and toss lightly. Serve at once.

Makes 6 servings.

## GOSSAMER SALAD

Gourmets will regard this salad as a superb delicacy.

SALAD:

Salad greens
9 hard-cooked eggs, quartered
1 large avocado, sliced

2 medium-sized tomatoes,
sliced

DRESSING:

1 cup mayonnaise
¼ cup catsup
1 hard-cooked egg, finely
chopped

2 tablespoons chopped ripe
olives
1 teaspoon minced chives
1 teaspoon lemon juice

*Salad:* Line salad bowl with crisp greens. Heap eggs on greens and circle with avocado slices and tomato slices. Sprinkle with salt. Serve with dressing.
*Dressing:* Combine all dressing ingredients. Chill.
Makes 6 servings.

## LUSCIOUS STUFFED TOMATOES

Try this summer's day luncheon salad.

4 medium-sized tomatoes
1 3-ounce package cream
cheese
1 small avocado, mashed

½ teaspoon salt
Grated onion
Dash Tabasco sauce

Peel tomatoes and remove cores. Place on garnished plates. Cut each tomato part way through into 6 wedges. Spread wedges apart. Soften cream cheese with a fork. Blend avocado into cream cheese. Add salt, onion to taste, and Tabasco sauce. Heap into centers of tomatoes.
Makes 4 servings.

## MEXICALI SALAD

For that South of the Border flavor, serve this.

⅓ cup salad oil
2 tablespoons wine vinegar
½ teaspoon salt
Dash pepper
Dash Tabasco sauce
2 tablespoons chopped canned
  green chilies

2 tablespoons chopped
  pimiento
1 large avocado, diced
2 large red tomatoes,
  chopped

Combine oil, vinegar, and seasonings in jar. Cover and shake vigorously. Add chilies and pimiento. Combine avocado and tomatoes. Pour dressing over salad. Spoon onto garnished salad plates.
Makes 4 or 5 servings.

## PACIFIC CABBAGE SLAW

Serve this easily made tossed salad.

3 cups shredded cabbage
2 tablespoons minced green
  pepper
2 tablespoons slivered
  pimiento
⅓ cup dairy sour cream

2 tablespoons vinegar
1 tablespoon sugar
Cayenne pepper
1 medium-sized avocado,
  diced
Salt to taste

Combine cabbage, green pepper, and pimiento. Blend sour cream, vinegar, sugar, and a dash cayenne. Blend with cabbage mixture. Chill. Just before serving add avocado. Salt to taste and mix together lightly.
Makes 5 or 6 servings.

## PASADENA HOLIDAY SALAD

Your holiday dinner will be memorable when you serve this.

| | |
|---|---|
| 2 medium-sized avocados | ¼ cup finely chopped celery |
| Fresh lemon juice | ⅔ cup tomato cocktail sauce |
| Salt | ⅓ cup mayonnaise |
| 1 8-ounce can cut asparagus spears | Dash Tabasco sauce |

Halve and seed avocados. Sprinkle with lemon juice and salt. Arrange avocado halves on garnished plates and fill with asparagus. Combine celery, cocktail sauce, mayonnaise, 1 tablespoon lemon juice, and Tabasco sauce. Pour over asparagus.

Makes 4 servings.

## PATIO SALAD

For something different and colorful in a vegetable salad, make this.

| | |
|---|---|
| 3 large avocados | 1 16-ounce can green beans |
| Lemon juice | 1 8-ounce can sliced pickled beets |
| Salt | |
| French dressing | |

Halve, seed, and peel avocados. Sprinkle with lemon juice and salt. Pour French dressing over green beans. Cut beets into strips. Add to green beans. Place avocado halves on garnished salad plates and heap with vegetable mixture.

Makes 6 servings.

*Avocado Lucky Salad.* This salad not only looks stunning but tastes good and pleases all age groups. (page 91)

*Chicken Livers Superba in Avocado Shells* makes a meal memorable. For this delicious entree, heat avocado halves and fill with hot chicken livers in sour cream sauce, topped with avocado balls. (page 148)

11

*Crab Acapulco,* lovely to look at, delightful to eat, is a savory combination of crab meat in subtly flavored avocado half-shells. (page 154)

## POTPOURRI TOSSUP

A well-seasoned salad is this.

4 cups mixed salad greens
1 green onion, thinly sliced
3 tablespoons oil
Salt
Pepper
1 medium-sized avocado,
    diced

1 medium-sized tomato
1 tablespoon wine vinegar
6 to 8 cooked asparagus
    spears

Break salad greens into bite-sized pieces. Add onion. Sprinkle with oil and salt and pepper to taste. Toss lightly. Add avocado. Cut tomato into wedges and add to mixture. Sprinkle avocado and tomato with salt, add vinegar, and toss again very lightly. Garnish with asparagus spears.

Makes 4 to 6 servings.

## RED AND GREEN SALAD

When you need a colorful salad for a holiday season, use this one.

2 medium-sized avocados
Fresh lemon juice
Salt
½ cup julienne cut cooked
    beets

½ cup finely chopped celery
French dressing
2 hard-cooked eggs, quartered

Halve and seed avocados. Sprinkle with lemon juice and salt. Combine beets and celery, and toss with French dressing. Place half-shells on garnished salad plates and fill with vegetable mixture. Garnish with hard-cooked eggs.

Makes 4 servings.

## SAN RAFAEL SALAD BOWL

Here is a salad that could be a whole supper on hot days.

**SALAD:**

*1 small head lettuce*
*2 hard-cooked eggs, diced*
*1 green onion, sliced*
*1 medium-sized avocado,*
*   diced*

*½ medium-sized cucumber,*
*   sliced*
*½ cup diced American*
*   cheese*

**DRESSING:**

*¼ cup salad oil*
*1½ tablespoons wine vinegar*
*1 teaspoon salt*

*Dash pepper*
*2 tablespoons mayonnaise*

*Salad:* Break lettuce into bite-sized pieces. Add eggs. Sprinkle onion, avocado, cucumber, and cheese over lettuce.

*Dressing:* Blend oil, vinegar, salt and pepper. Add mayonnaise and beat with a fork until well blended. Sprinkle over salad mixture and toss lightly to blend. Serve at once. Makes 6 servings.

## SUMMER VEGETABLE SALAD

Brighten your life with this salad.

*1 cup grated carrot*
*½ cup finely chopped celery*
*2 tablespoons chopped green*
*   pepper*
*½ teaspoon salt*

*¼ cup mayonnaise*
*1 teaspoon fresh lemon juice*
*1 medium-sized avocado,*
*   diced*

Combine carrot, celery, and green pepper with salt, mayonnaise, and lemon juice. Stir lightly to blend. Add avocado to salad mixture and mix lightly. Serve on garnished salad plates. Makes 4 servings.

## SUNBURST SALAD

This salad is pretty enough for a special luncheon party.

| | |
|---|---|
| 2 medium-sized avocados | 2 tablespoons chopped dill |
| Fresh lemon juice | pickle |
| Salt | 1 tablespoon minced onion |
| Salad greens | 1 teaspoon prepared mustard |
| 4 hard-cooked eggs, diced | Mayonnaise |
| ¼ cup chopped pimiento | Pepper |
| ½ cup finely chopped celery | 6 ripe olives |
| | French dressing |

Halve, seed, peel, and slice avocados. Sprinkle avocado slices
with lemon juice and salt and arrange in sunburst fashion on
salad greens. Combine eggs, pimiento, celery, pickle, onion, mustard, and enough mayonnaise to moisten. Season with salt and
pepper; mix lightly. Spoon mound of egg mixture over avocado
slices. Garnish with ripe olives and serve with French dressing.
Makes 6 servings.

## WESTERN COLESLAW

Be sure to serve this budget salad often.

| | |
|---|---|
| 2 medium-sized avocados | Salt |
| French dressing | 3 cups finely shredded |
| Lettuce | cabbage |
| 6 tablespoons mayonnaise | 1 cup grated carrot |
| 1 teaspoon Worcestershire | |
| sauce | |

Halve, seed, and peel avocados. Cut fruit into quarters lengthwise. Dress avocado with French dressing. Arrange avocado quarters and lettuce on four salad plates. Combine mayonnaise, Worcestershire sauce, and salt to taste. Blend with cabbage and carrot.
Serve over avocado quarters.
Makes 4 servings.

# "QUICKIE" IDEAS

### FRUIT

Looking for a new winter salad that's festive? Alternate grapefruit sections with ripe tomato quarters on crisp lettuce. Top with mashed avocado seasoned with instant minced onion, salt, and fresh lemon juice.

Nothing can add so much to a green salad as cubes of mellow avocado and a fresh lemon juice dressing.

Mellow-flavored slices of pale green avocado make a beautiful and refreshing salad when they're arranged on salad plates with fresh orange segments and crisp Tokay grapes. Serve with French dressing or your favorite fruit salad dressing.

Fill mellow, pale green avocado halves with sweetened berries and top with a spoonful of tangy dairy sour cream to make a delicious and easy summer fruit salad.

Make an attractive help-yourself salad for a buffet by arranging avocado halves in a ring on a large platter and heaping the centers with sliced fresh fruit.

For pretty party luncheon salads, use avocado half-shells filled with bite-sized pieces of fruit in season. Serve with fresh lemon or lime juice.

### MEAT

Combine diced ham or chicken, a little fresh lemon juice, diced celery and mayonnaise with salt and pepper to taste; heap into avocado half-shells. Arrange on crisp beds of lettuce.

Mix diced ham with finely chopped celery, capers, and mayonnaise. Serve in an avocado half-shell for a marvelous main dish salad.

### POULTRY

An excellent chicken salad combines halved, seeded grapes, avocado cubes, and finely chopped celery with diced chicken. Serve in lettuce cups with finger sandwiches and whole spiced peaches.

### SEAFOOD

*Party salad:* Arrange fresh or canned crab meat and sliced avocado on shredded lettuce; garnish with quartered hard-cooked eggs, tomato wedges, and ripe olives. Serve with French dressing.

*Surprise half-shells:* Scoop the fruit out of the half-shell with a sharp large spoon; gently turn the peeled half-shell over with the round side on top. Under it place a few pieces of lobster or other seafood; top with a sour cream dressing and a strip of pimiento.

### VEGETABLE

For an Easter dinner, serve this handsome gold and green salad prepared with slices of avocado arranged pinwheel fashion on salad greens with a topping of mayonnaise and hard-cooked egg, sieved.

Add cubed avocado to coleslaw for added color and flavor.

Put a deviled egg in a peeled avocado half-shell; top with mayonnaise. Another way is to fill the cup with cold marinated cucumbers.

*Italian Salad:* Marinate cooked asparagus with Italian salad dressing. Serve on salad greens with avocado crescents and pimento strips; drizzle with Italian dressing.

# SALAD DRESSINGS

A tangy, zesty dressing can give flavor to even the blandest of salads. Avocados, with their special flavor, enhance any combination of ingredients in salad dressings. Also, a salad dressing properly prepared can complement an avocado salad and make it a taste delight. Some salad dressings are just for fruits; others for vegetables, meats, seafood, and poultry. A salad dressing can be an adventure for the hostess and the diner alike.

## AVOCADO BLUE CHEESE DRESSING

If you are fond of blue cheese, you will like this particular dressing.

*1 large avocado, mashed*
*½ cup mayonnaise*

*½ teaspoon salt*
*¼ cup crumbled blue cheese*

Blend avocado with remaining ingredients.
Makes about 1½ cups.

## AVOCADO CHEESE DRESSING

Avocado and cottage cheese make a delightfully different dressing.

*1 small avocado*
*½ cup small-curd cottage cheese*
*¼ cup vinegar*
*1½ tablespoons sugar*
*1 teaspoon salt*

*Dash dry mustard*
*Dash pepper*
*Dash Tabasco sauce*
*¼ teaspoon grated onion*
*¼ cup salad oil*

Mash avocado, add cottage cheese, and beat well with rotary beater. Stir in vinegar, sugar, salt, mustard, pepper, Tabasco, and onion. Gradually blend in oil. If dressing is too thick, stir in a tablespoon of cold water.

Makes about 1½ cups.

## AVOCADO FRENCH DRESSING

Here's a variation that is sure to please.

½ cup salad oil
2 tablespoons fresh lemon
   juice
1 teaspoon sugar
½ teaspoon salt
Dash pepper

Dash cayenne
½ cup mashed avocado
2 tablespoons grated carrot
2 tablespoons finely chopped
   celery

Blend all ingredients together.
Makes about 1⅓ cups.

## AVOCADO FRUIT DELIGHT DRESSING

This dressing is just for fruit and is, oh, so good.

1 large avocado
¾ cup orange juice
2 tablespoons lemon juice
2 tablespoons honey
½ teaspoon salt

Mash avocado. Gradually add remaining ingredients. Beat thoroughly. Chill.

Makes about 1½ cups.

## AVOCADO ROQUEFORT DRESSING

Roquefort dressing pleases many. Now add avocado.

*1 medium-sized avocado*
*½ cup salad oil*
*¼ cup fresh lemon juice*
*1 teaspoon salt*

*1 tablespoon wine vinegar*
*Few drops Tabasco sauce*
*2 tablespoons crumbled*
*Roquefort cheese*

Force avocado through a sieve. Blend oil, lemon juice, salt, vinegar, and Tabasco into avocado. Fold in cheese. Serve over salad greens.

Makes about 1½ cups.

## AVOCADO SOUR CREAM DRESSING

Tangy dressings such as this are delicious.

*1 small avocado*
*¼ cup dairy sour cream*
*3 tablespoons fresh lemon*
*   juice*

*1 teaspoon sugar*
*¼ teaspoon salt*
*Few grains cayenne pepper*
*Dash Tabasco sauce*

Force avocado through sieve. Combine all ingredients and blend thoroughly.

Makes about 1 cup.

## AVOCADO THOUSAND ISLAND DRESSING

Here is a truly new dressing that you'll relish.

*1 small avocado, mashed*
*½ cup mayonnaise*
*1 hard-cooked egg, diced*
*2 tablespoons undrained*
  *pickle relish*

*3 tablespoons chopped ripe*
  *olives*
*½ teaspoon salt*

Combine all ingredients and mix well. Serve on a head of lettuce.
Makes about 1½ cups.

## CALIFORNIA FRENCH DRESSING

Here's an extra good dressing for fruit salads.

*1 small avocado, sieved*
*¼ cup fresh lemon juice*

*¼ cup salad oil*
*1 teaspoon salt*

Blend all ingredients together. Serve on citrus fruit salads.
Makes about 1 cup

## DEL MAR DRESSING

Enjoy this tropical flavor in salad dressing.

*1 small avocado, sieved*
*½ cup pineapple juice*
*3 tablespoons fresh lemon*
  *juice*

*½ teaspoon salt*
*Few drops Tabasco sauce*

Blend all ingredients together. Serve on fruit salads.
Makes about ¾ cup.

## PARSLEY AVOCADO DRESSING

Parsley contributes to fine flavor in this dressing.

1 small avocado, sieved
¼ cup mayonnaise
2 tablespoons fresh lemon
  juice
¼ cup tomato juice

½ teaspoon grated onion
Few drops Worcestershire
  sauce
1 teaspoon salt
¼ cup chopped parsley

Blend together all ingredients. Serve on green salads or with fish salads.

Makes about 1¼ cups dressing.

## "QUICKIE" IDEA

Give yourself about 2 minutes to make this "magic mayonnaise." Put into the blender or use a rotary beater, a peeled medium-sized avocado, ¼ cup salad oil, 1 egg, juice of 1 small lemon, ½ teaspoon salt, ¼ teaspoon prepared mustard and whir for just a few seconds, not too long. Keep the mixture chilled; use it instead of regular mayonnaise. Mix it with potato salad or over fruit salad. Use it as a shrimp dip. (Important: It has about half the calories of mayonnaise!)

# Entrees

"All human history attests
That happiness for man—the hungry sinner!
Since Eve ate apples, much depends on dinner!"

—Lord Byron, *Don Juan*

An entree is meant to be exactly what its name implies—an entrance, and, when applied to food, an introduction to a repast. It is also the main dish of an informal meal or any food served as the main dish of the meal (French—*pièce de résistance*). Avocado entrees provide new adventures in eating. If you have not tasted the rich goodness of warm avocado as suggested in these entrees, a gourmet's treat awaits you. Even leftover food can be transformed into company fare.

## MEAT ENTREES

### Bacon

### AVOCADO RICE RING

This is an entree that should score a hit with family or guests.

| | |
|---|---|
| 6 strips bacon | 2 teaspoons lemon juice |
| 1 8-ounce can tomato sauce | ¼ cup water |
| 1 16-ounce can tomatoes | ¾ cup grated Cheddar |
| 2 tablespoons grated onion | cheese |
| ¼ teaspoon salt | 6 cups hot cooked rice |
| ½ teaspoon chili powder | 2 medium-sized avocados |

Fry bacon crisp; drain and crumble. Pour off drippings and into same pan put tomato sauce, tomatoes, onion, salt, chili powder,

1 teaspoon lemon juice, and water. Simmer about 10 minutes. Combine cheese with half of tomato mixture; mix with cooked rice. Pack into 1½-quart ring mold. Keep hot in a 350° oven. Cube 1 avocado; carefully add to remainder of tomato sauce mixture. Slice other avocado; cut into rather thick slices and sprinkle with remaining lemon juice. Loosen rice from sides of ring mold and place on hot serving platter. Garnish with avocado slices by placing them stem side up around outside edge of rice ring. Serve with hot tomato-avocado sauce.

Makes 8 to 10 servings.

## AVOCADO LOS ALAMOS

The heat of the sauce brings out the delicate flavor of the avocado.

| | |
|---|---|
| ¼ cup tomato catsup | Salt and pepper to taste |
| ¼ cup vinegar | 2 tablespoons sugar |
| ¼ cup butter or margarine | 4 strips bacon |
| 1 tablespoon Worcestershire sauce | 3 medium-sized avocados |

Combine catsup, vinegar, butter or margarine, Worcestershire sauce, salt, pepper, and sugar in top of double boiler; keep hot until serving time. Meanwhile, cook bacon crisp, drain, and crumble. Halve and seed avocados; do not peel. Put crumbled bacon into each half-shell and pour hot sauce over all. If more sauce is needed, recipe can be doubled and served in separate dish at the table.

Makes 6 servings.

## *Beef*

### AVOCADO HALF-SHELL MACÉDOINE

A zesty avocado filling makes this meat entree a special favorite.

| | |
|---|---|
| 2 medium-sized avocados | ½ cup sliced fresh or canned |
| Salt | mushrooms |
| 1 cup tomato sauce | 2 tablespoons minced parsley |
| ½ teaspoon chili powder | 2 tablespoons minced onion |
| ½ cup cubed cooked beef | Toasted, buttered bread |
| | crumbs |

Halve and seed avocados; sprinkle salt on half-shells. Combine tomato sauce, chili powder, salt to taste, beef, mushrooms, parsley, and onion; heat to boiling. Place avocado half-shells in shallow pan containing ¼-inch warm water. Fill shells with beef mixture and sprinkle with bread crumbs. Bake in a 325° oven for 15 minutes. Serve immediately.

Makes 4 servings.

### AVOCADO HALF-SHELL MEXICALI

Here is an entree that is simple to make but very distinctive.

| | |
|---|---|
| 3 medium-sized avocados | Grated sharp American |
| Salt | cheese |
| 2 cups canned chili con | Finely chopped onion |
| carne (no beans) | (optional) |

Halve and seed avocados; sprinkle half-shells with salt. Heat chili con carne to boiling. Arrange avocado half-shells in shallow pan containing ¼-inch warm water. Fill shells with chili con carne. Bake in a 325° oven for 15 minutes. Remove from oven; sprinkle each serving with cheese and onion (optional).

Makes 6 servings.

## LOS ALTOS CREAMED BEEF

Here's an easy-to-do entree with canned soup, beef, and avocado.

½ pound lean ground beef
1 tablespoon cooking oil
3 tablespoons chopped onion
½ teaspoon salt
1 10½-ounce can condensed
cream of celery or cream of
vegetable soup

½ cup milk
1 large avocado
Hot cooked rice or toast
triangles

Brown beef in oil. Add onion and salt when meat is partially cooked. When meat is well-browned, stir in soup and milk; simmer for 5 minutes. Cube avocado and stir into sauce. Heat for only 1 or 2 minutes and serve over hot rice or toast triangles. Makes 6 servings.

## MEAT BALLS STROGANOFF À LA AVOCADO

Here is a one-dish meal that hits the spot where the budget is concerned.

1 cup bread crumbs
⅓ cup milk
¼ cup finely chopped onion
1 pound lean ground beef
1 egg, slightly beaten
1 teaspoon salt
Dash pepper
½ teaspoon nutmeg

2 tablespoons butter or
margarine
1 10½-ounce can cream of
mushroom soup
1 cup dairy sour cream
3 medium-sized avocados
3 cups hot cooked rice
Minced parsley
Paprika

Moisten crumbs in milk. Put together with onion, beef, egg, seasonings and mix well. Shape into 30 balls (about 1 inch each). Melt butter or margarine in pan; fry meat balls. Remove meat from pan; remove excess fat. Into pan put soup and sour cream;

return meat balls, cover and heat well but do not boil. Halve, seed, and peel avocados. Spoon hot rice onto serving platter; arrange avocado halves on top. Put 5 meat balls into each avocado half and cover with soup-sour cream mixture. Garnish with minced parsley and paprika.

Makes 6 servings.

## SOUTH OF THE BORDER AVOCADO

Ole! Serve a unique entree with a Mexican touch.

| | |
|---|---|
| 1 small onion, finely chopped | 1 teaspoon chili powder |
| 1 small garlic clove, minced | 1½ teaspoons salt |
| ¼ cup salad oil | 1 16-ounce can red kidney |
| ¾ pound lean ground beef | beans |
| 1 16-ounce can tomatoes | 3 medium-sized avocados |

Cook onion and garlic slowly in oil until tender. Add beef and brown well. Add tomatoes, chili powder, salt, and undrained kidney beans. Simmer 15 minutes, stirring occasionally. Halve and seed avocados. Place a half-shell on each serving plate and spoon chili mixture into each shell. Serve at once.

Makes 6 servings.

## *Chipped Beef*

## AVOCADO DEL MAR

Creamed chipped beef becomes something special in this entree.

| | |
|---|---|
| ¼ pound thinly sliced chipped beef | 2 cups milk |
| | 1 medium-sized avocado |
| 6 tablespoons butter or margarine | Fresh lemon or lime juice |
| | Salt |
| 6 tablespoons flour | 6 slices toast |

Shred chipped beef. Melt butter or margarine, blend in flour, and stir in milk. Cook and stir until mixture is thickened. Stir in chipped beef and heat thoroughly. Cut avocado into slices and sprinkle with lemon or lime juice and salt. Pour creamed chipped beef over toast and top each serving with 2 or 3 avocado slices. Serve at once.

Makes 6 servings.


## CHIPPED BEEF, ELITE

This may be just what you want for an unusual luncheon main dish.

| | |
|---|---|
| 3 tablespoons butter | 1 cup table cream |
| ¼ pound chipped beef | 1 teaspoon Worcestershire |
| 1 tablespoon instant minced | sauce |
| onion | 2 tablespoons chopped |
| 2 tablespoons slivered green | pimiento |
| pepper | 1 cup cooked green peas, |
| 2 tablespoons flour | drained |
| 1 10½-ounce can cream of | 3 medium-sized avocados |
| mushroom soup | Lemon juice |

Melt butter in skillet. Tear chipped beef into bite-sized pieces and cook slightly in butter until edges begin to frizzle. Add onion and green pepper; blend in flour. Add undiluted soup and cream; cook until thickened, stirring constantly. Stir in Worcestershire sauce, pimiento, and peas. Halve and seed avocados. Sprinkle half-shells with a little lemon juice. Spoon hot chipped beef mixture into avocado half-shells and serve.

Makes 6 servings.

## Corned Beef

### CORNED BEEF HASH, WESTERN WAY

You'll be surprised when you try out this entree and discover its unusual flavor combination.

3 slices bacon
3 cups cold diced boiled
   potatoes
1 12-ounce can corned beef
1 tablespoon finely chopped
   onion

1 10½-ounce can condensed
   vegetable soup
1 medium-sized avocado
Salt
Parsley

Fry bacon until crisp, drain, and crumble; mix with potatoes, corned beef, onion, and soup. Fry this mixture slowly until a brown crust is formed on bottom. Cut avocado into slices; sprinkle with salt. Turn out corned beef hash onto platter and make slashes in top of the mixture. Insert avocado slices into slashes. Place in a 325° oven for about 5 minutes. Serve with parsley garnish.

Makes 6 to 8 servings.

## Frankfurters

### AVOCADO SPANISH FRANKFURTER

Try this entree next time you have some hungry young people present.

3 medium-sized avocados
Salt
4 all-meat frankfurters
1 tablespoon cooking oil
¾ cup tomato juice
⅓ cup chopped ripe olives

½ teaspoon garlic salt
1 tablespoon flour
1 teaspoon chili powder
¼ cup water
3 tablespoons finely chopped
   onion (optional)

Halve and seed avocados; sprinkle half-shells with salt. Slice frankfurters crosswise; sauté slightly in oil. Blend tomato juice, olives, and garlic salt together and heat to boiling. Make a paste of flour, chili powder, and water and blend into tomato juice mixture. Cook and stir for 3 minutes. Stir in frankfurter pieces. Arrange avocados on serving plates. Heap half-shells with hot tomato-frankfurter mixture. Sprinkle with chopped onion if desired. Makes 6 servings.

## FAMILY FRANKS

This is a quick, nutritious family supper dish or for Saturday lunch.

| | |
|---|---|
| 1 16-ounce can green lima beans | 1/4 cup finely chopped onion |
| 2 tablespoons butter or margarine | 1 teaspoon chili powder |
| | 6 all-meat frankfurters |
| | 1 medium-sized avocado |

Heat undrained lima beans with butter or margarine, onion, chili powder; stir well. Slit frankfurters lengthwise halfway through. Cut avocado into 6 slices and fit avocado slices into frankfurters. Place frankfurters into pan with lima beans, cover and heat through. Makes 6 servings.

## *Ham*

## AVOCADO HALF-SHELL, ENCINITAS

For a satisfying, different, and delicious combination, try this.

| | |
|---|---|
| 3 medium-sized avocados | 1 cup cubed cooked ham |
| Salt | Buttered, toasted bread |
| 1 cup tomato sauce | crumbs |
| 1/2 teaspoon chili powder | Parsley |

Halve and seed avocados. Sprinkle half-shells with salt. Combine tomato sauce, chili powder, and ham; heat to boiling point. Place half-shells in shallow pan containing 1/4-inch warm water.

Fill with ham mixture. Bake in a 325° oven for 15 minutes. Remove from oven; sprinkle tops with bread crumbs and a sprig of parsley; serve at once.

Makes 6 servings.

## AVOCADO HAM SAVORY

For Sunday-night supper, serve an appetite-teasing sauce on hot biscuits or waffles.

| | |
|---|---|
| 1 large avocado | ¼ cup flour |
| Salt | 2 cups milk |
| 1 cup cubed cooked ham | Hot biscuits or waffles |

Cube avocado; sprinkle with little salt. Fry ham until slightly brown. Mix flour with small amount of milk to make a paste. Pour remaining milk over browned ham and allow to simmer a few minutes. Stir in flour mixture and cook until thickened. Add avocado cubes just before serving; do not cook. Serve over fluffy hot biscuits or small waffles.

Makes 4 to 5 servings.

## AVOCADO LUNCHEON SCALLOP

With this hearty entree, you need only toast, a green salad, and a beverage.

| | |
|---|---|
| 2 medium-sized avocados | ⅓ cup diced canned |
| Salt | pimiento |
| 3 tablespoons butter or | 1½ cups diced cooked or |
| margarine | canned asparagus |
| 3 tablespoons flour | 1 cup diced cooked ham |
| 1½ cups milk | |

Halve and seed avocados; sprinkle half-shells with salt. Melt butter or margarine; blend in flour and a little salt. Add milk and stir until sauce is thickened. Add pimiento, asparagus, and cubed ham. Put avocado half-shells in shallow pan containing ¼-inch warm water. Fill each one with asparagus-ham mixture. Bake in a 325° oven for 15 minutes. Serve immediately.

Makes 4 servings.

## FIRESIDE SPAGHETTI

Here's an easy top-of-the-stove luncheon dish keyed to family tastes.

| | |
|---|---|
| *1 large slice ham* | *Dash Worcestershire sauce* |
| *¼ cup finely chopped green* | *Salt* |
| *pepper* | *6 servings cooked spaghetti* |
| *2 tablespoons flour* | *1 medium-sized avocado* |
| *1⅔ cups milk* | *Paprika* |

Cut ham into cubes and fry until slightly browned. Add green pepper and cook about 1 minute. Blend in flour; add milk and cook and stir until mixture thickens. Add Worcestershire sauce, salt to taste, and cooked spaghetti; heat to boiling. Cube avocado; sprinkle with salt. Lightly stir avocado cubes into hot spaghetti mixture. Pour into serving platter; sprinkle with paprika.

Makes 6 servings.

## HAM AVOCADO SUPERB

This is a frankly fancy but delicious and substantial entree.

| | |
|---|---|
| *¼ cup butter or margarine* | *½ teaspoon Worcestershire* |
| *¼ cup flour* | *sauce* |
| *2 cups table cream* | *8 slices white sandwich bread* |
| *2 cups diced cooked ham* | *4 medium-sized avocados* |
| *½ cup finely chopped celery* | *Salt* |
| *1 teaspoon grated onion* | *⅔ cup grated sharp* |
| | *American cheese* |

Melt butter or margarine; add flour and gradually blend in cream, stirring constantly over heat just below boiling. Reduce heat, stir, and cook sauce for about 15 minutes (it will be very thick). Add ham, celery, onion, and Worcestershire sauce. Blend well and keep warm over very slow heat. Toast bread and trim crusts. On cookie sheet or in shallow pan, place toast and atop each put an avocado half that has been peeled and slightly salted. Spoon ham mixture into each avocado half-shell and over toast. Cover toast completely so that it does not become brown when broiled. Broil for 3 to 4 minutes about 5 or 6 inches from broiler heat. Remove from broiler; sprinkle with cheese and broil about a minute longer, until cheese is slightly brown and bubbly. Serve very hot.

Makes 8 servings.

## Veal

### AVOCADO HALF-SHELL SCALLOP

Your family will never suspect that this entree is made from leftovers.

4 medium-sized avocados  
Salt  
¾ cup canned whole kernel corn  
¾ cup cubed cooked veal  
½ cup finely chopped celery  
3 tablespoons milk  
Paprika  
Toasted bread crumbs

Halve avocados, remove seeds, and sprinkle with salt. Combine corn, veal, celery, milk, salt to taste, and paprika and heat to boiling. Place avocado half-shells in shallow pan containing ¼-inch warm water. Fill each shell with meat mixture. Heat in a 325° oven for 15 minutes. Remove from heat and sprinkle with bread crumbs. Serve at once.

Makes 8 servings.

## SUPER-DUPER VEAL

Hot buttered noodles are ideal with this party fare.

1½ pounds lean veal
2 tablespoons cooking oil
1 6-ounce can sliced
    mushrooms
⅓ cup white table wine or
    2½ tablespoons each lemon
    juice and water

¼ cup finely chopped onion
½ teaspoon salt
¼ teaspoon orégano
1 cup dairy sour cream
2 tablespoons cornstarch
2 tablespoons water
3 medium-sized avocados

Cut veal into 1-inch cubes; brown in oil. Drain mushroom liquid into measuring cup; add enough water to make 1 cup. Add to veal together with wine or lemon juice and water, onion, salt, and orégano. Cover and simmer until veal is tender, about 1 hour. Just before serving, add mushrooms and sour cream. Blend cornstarch and water; stir into mixture. Heat just until thickened. Halve, seed, and peel avocados. Fill each half-shell with veal mixture. Serve very hot.

Makes 6 servings.

# POULTRY ENTREES

## *Chicken*

### AVOCADO À LA POULETTE

Serve this main dish to prove that you are an imaginative cook.

½ 8½-ounce can cream of
  chicken soup
2 tablespoons mayonnaise
1 teaspoon Worcestershire
  sauce
1 5-ounce can boned chicken

1 8-ounce can peas or 1 cup
  cooked peas
2 medium-sized avocados
2 teaspoons lemon juice
1 tablespoon slivered toasted
  almonds

Stir together soup, mayonnaise, Worcestershire sauce, chicken
and peas; heat well. Halve and seed avocados; brush with lemon
juice. When ready to serve, fill each half-shell with the chicken
mixture and sprinkle with almonds.

Makes 4 servings.

### AVOCADO-CHICKEN BON VIVANT

This could easily be one of the most impressive luncheon entrees
you have ever served.

2 tablespoons butter
2 tablespoons flour
1 cup chicken broth
½ cup evaporated milk
1½ cups cooked chicken,
  diced

1 2-ounce can sliced
  mushrooms
Salt and pepper
2 medium-sized avocados
Pimientos, chopped

Melt butter, blend in flour, and gradually add broth and milk.
Cook until thickened. Add chicken, mushrooms, and seasonings.

Keep hot in top of double boiler. Halve, seed, and peel avocados. When ready to serve, spoon hot mixture into avocado halves and garnish with pimientos.

Makes 4 servings.

## AVOCADO MEXICALI

If you wish an excellent South of the Border entree, this is the answer.

3 medium-sized avocados
Salt
½ cup chopped ripe olives
1 cup diced cooked chicken

1 cup tomato sauce
¼ teaspoon garlic salt
1 teaspoon chili powder
Chopped parsley

Halve and seed avocados; sprinkle half-shells with salt. Combine chopped olives, diced chicken, tomato sauce, garlic salt, chili powder and boil 2 or 3 minutes. Place half-shells in shallow pan containing ¼-inch warm water. Fill each shell with chicken-tomato mixture and bake in a 325° oven for 15 minutes. Garnish with chopped parsley. Makes 6 servings.

## CHICKEN AVOCADO À L'ORANGE

Be the one to serve guests the most unusual dinner dish they have ever tasted.

⅓ cup flour
1½ teaspoons salt
Dash pepper
¾ teaspoon curry powder
1 teaspoon chili powder
1 2-pound chicken, cut in
    pieces
¾ cup melted butter

2 cups orange juice
1 tablespoon grated orange
    rind
1 cup pecan halves
2 to 2½ cups cooked rice
1 medium-sized avocado,
    sliced
1 medium-sized orange, sliced

Put flour, salt, pepper, curry powder, and chili powder in paper bag. Dip chicken pieces in melted butter, drop them in bag and

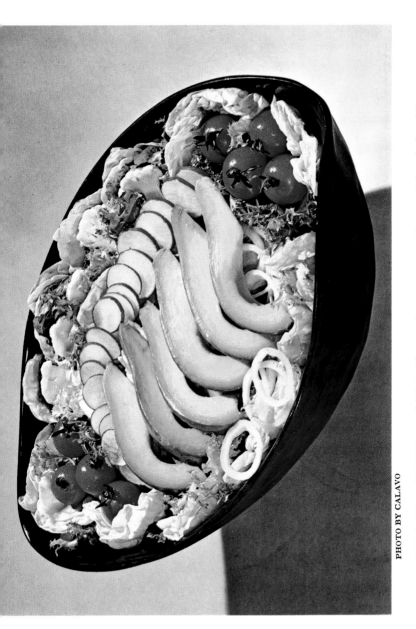

*Salad—Unmolded (Vegetable)*. Add avocado to any special vegetable salad and listen to the plaudits.

13

coat pieces with flour by shaking them in bag. Broil or fry chicken in remaining butter until well done. Meanwhile, blend flour left in bag with orange juice and heat until thickened. Stir in orange rind and pecan halves. Arrange rice on serving platter and pour most of orange sauce over rice. Place avocado slices and orange slices in a row down the middle of the rice. Place chicken pieces along each side of the center. Spoon remaining sauce over avocado and orange slices.

Makes 6 to 8 servings.

## CHICKEN-AVOCADO PERFECTION

Choose this buffet entree because it is both delicious and ample.

*6 pounds chicken, fryers*
*4 cups water*
*4 stalks celery*
*1 small onion*
*Salt and pepper*
*2 tablespoons butter*
*3 tablespoons flour*
*1 cup chicken stock*
*1 cup table cream*
*½ cup grated sharp American cheese*

*Dash Tabasco sauce*
*¼ teaspoon each rosemary and basil*
*1 4-ounce can sliced mushrooms*
*2 medium-sized avocados, diced*
*½ cup slivered toasted almonds*

Boil chicken pieces in water with celery, onion, salt and pepper to taste; simmer until chicken is tender. Remove from broth, cool, and remove meat from bones of all pieces but wings and necks. Return bones, necks, and wings to chicken stock and simmer for ½ hour longer. Melt butter in saucepan; blend in flour and stir in 1 cup chicken stock and 1 cup cream. Stir until thickened; add cheese, salt, Tabasco sauce, and herbs. In bottom of casserole or shallow baking dish, put layer of chicken chunks, then layer of sautéed mushrooms. Sprinkle lightly with salt and pepper. Pour sauce over chicken and bake in a 350° oven for 25 minutes. Remove from oven; carefully add diced avocado to chicken mixture. Return covered casserole to oven and bake for 10 to 15 minutes longer. Just before serving, garnish with almonds.

Makes 8 to 10 servings.

## CHICKEN LIVERS SUPERBA

This unusual entree in half-shells glamorizes any buffet or guest luncheon.

2 medium-sized avocados
Fresh lemon juice
¾ pound chicken livers
2 tablespoons butter
1½ tablespoons flour
¼ teaspoon salt
Dash pepper

¾ cup chicken stock or 2
chicken bouillon cubes
dissolved in hot water
½ cup dairy sour cream
1 tablespoon white dinner
wine

Halve and seed avocados; brush halves with a little lemon juice. Place half-shells in shallow baking dish containing ¼-inch warm water. Heat in a 300° oven until heated through. Slowly brown chicken livers in butter. Stir in flour, salt and pepper. Gradually add chicken stock or bouillon; cook and stir until thickened. Blend in sour cream, wine, and 1 teaspoon lemon juice; heat through. Spoon chicken liver mixture into heated half-shells and serve.

Makes 4 servings.

## CHICKEN VIRTUOSO

To impress guests with your reputation as a good cook, try this!

2 frying chickens
4 cups water
1 small onion
1 carrot
2 stalks celery
1 bay leaf, pinch each of
rosemary and thyme
4 tablespoons butter

3 tablespoons flour
2 cups strained chicken stock
½ cup dairy sour cream
2 tablespoons white sherry
(optional)
Salt and pepper
2 medium-sized avocados
Paprika

Boil chicken pieces in water with onion, carrot, celery, and seasonings until chicken is tender. Remove from broth and when cool, remove bones. Keep in serving-size pieces as much as possible. Melt butter, blend in flour, and slowly add chicken stock. Cook and stir until thickened, then add sour cream and sherry, if desired, salt and pepper to taste. Cut each avocado in 4 lengthwise pieces; remove seed and skin. Arrange chicken pieces on hot platter with the avocado slices on top. Pour sauce over all; sprinkle with paprika and serve piping hot. If for a buffet, use 4 boned whole chicken breasts, split into 8 pieces and follow the same method of preparation.

Makes 8 servings.

## CHICKEN WINDSOR

This is a favorite luncheon preparation for *femmes*.

*3 tablespoons butter*
*3 tablespoons flour*
*1 cup milk or chicken stock*
*½ teaspoon salt*
*2 cups diced cooked chicken*
*1 2-ounce can sliced*
*mushrooms*

*2 tablespoons chopped*
*pimientos*
*3 medium-sized avocados*
*1 4-ounce can jellied*
*cranberry sauce, diced*
*(optional)*

Melt butter; blend in flour. Add milk or chicken stock and salt; cook until mixture is thickened. Blend in chicken, drained mushrooms, and pimientos; keep hot over boiling water. Halve, peel, and seed avocados. Place half-shells in shallow pan containing ¼-inch warm water. Heat in a 300° oven for 15 minutes. Remove shells to serving dish and fill with chicken mixture. If desired, garnish with cranberry sauce.

Makes 6 servings.

## Turkey

### TURKEY CUM LAUDE

Leftover turkey becomes a party dish to praise when served in avocado half-shells.

4 slices bacon
1/4 cup chopped onion
1/2 cup finely sliced celery
1 10½-ounce can cream of
   chicken soup
Dash Worcestershire sauce

2 tablespoons grated
   Parmesan cheese
2 cups diced cooked turkey
   (or chicken)
3 small avocados
Crushed potato chips

Cut bacon into 1/4-inch strips and cook until crisp. Remove bacon but leave 2 tablespoons fat in the pan. Cook onion and celery in bacon fat until tender. Stir in undiluted soup, Worcestershire sauce and heat. Blend in cheese, turkey (or chicken), bacon bits; heat thoroughly. Halve, seed, and peel avocados. Place shells on individual serving plates and fill with turkey mixture. Sprinkle with crushed potato chips and serve at once.

Makes 6 servings.

### TURKEY EPICUREAN

You can prepare a memorable supper main dish with leftover turkey.

1 large avocado
Salt
1 10½-ounce can cream of
   celery soup
3 cups cooked noodles
1/4 cup chopped pimiento
2 tablespoons butter

1/2 teaspoon salt
2 cups diced cooked turkey
   (or chicken)
1/3 cup grated American
   cheese
Paprika

Cut avocado into cubes; sprinkle with little salt. Heat soup and stir in noodles, pimiento, butter, salt, and turkey (or chicken). When thoroughly heated, lightly stir in avocado cubes. Pour into buttered casserole, sprinkle with cheese and paprika; place under broiler to melt cheese, about 3 minutes. Serve immediately.

Makes 6 servings.

## TURKEY PARTY CASSEROLE

Here's a festive dish that's both economical and delicious.

| | |
|---|---|
| 4 tablespoons butter or margarine | Black pepper |
| | 1 chicken bouillon cube |
| 5 tablespoons flour | 2 cups cubed cooked turkey |
| 2 cups milk | 1 large avocado |
| ½ teaspoon salt | Lemon or lime juice |
| ½ teaspoon celery salt | Salt |
| ½ teaspoon dry mustard | ¼ cup slivered toasted almonds |
| Dash cayenne pepper | |

Melt butter or margarine and cook slowly until light brown. Blend in flour. Add milk, seasonings, and bouillon cube and cook and stir until thickened. Add turkey and simmer until thoroughly heated. Pour into shallow baking dish. Cut avocado into thin lengthwise slices. Sprinkle with little lemon or lime juice and salt. Arrange slices on top of casserole, pressing lightly into sauce. Sprinkle almonds around edge of dish. Heat about 5 minutes in a 350° oven. If desired, chicken may be substituted for turkey.

Makes 6 servings.

# SEAFOOD ENTREES

## *Clams*

### AVOCADO BARQUETTES

Sail into happy eating with these avocado half-shell boats!

| | |
|---|---|
| 2 tablespoons cooking oil | ½ pound fish fillet of choice |
| ¼ cup finely chopped onion | 1 4½-ounce can shrimp, |
| 1 teaspoon salt | drained |
| ¼ teaspoon thyme or | ¼ cup finely diced green |
| rosemary | pepper |
| ¼ teaspoon garlic salt | 4 small avocados |
| 1 7½-ounce can minced | Salt |
| clams | Hot rice for 8 servings |
| 1 16-ounce can tomatoes | |

Heat oil; add onion, salt, thyme or rosemary, garlic salt and cook for 5 minutes. Drain clams, reserving liquid. Stir clam liquid and tomatoes into onion mixture and simmer for 15 minutes. Cut fish fillet into 1-inch pieces; add to tomato mixture, together with clams, shrimp, and green pepper. Simmer together for 10 minutes. Halve, seed, and peel avocados. Sprinkle with a little salt. When ready to serve, place an avocado half-shell on each mound of rice and spoon seafood mixture over each avocado shell.

Makes 8 servings.

## AVOCADO CLAM SHELLS

Here's an entree you might find in a fancy restaurant, but you can have it at home.

3 tablespoons butter
1 teaspoon finely chopped
  onion
Pinch nutmeg
¼ cup flour
1 cup table cream or milk

2 teaspoons lemon juice
1 7½-ounce can clams
3 medium-sized avocados
Buttered bread crumbs
  (optional)

Simmer butter, onion, and nutmeg for few minutes. Stir in flour; blend in cream or milk and cook slowly until thickened. Blend in lemon juice. Add undrained clams and continue heating until ready to use. Halve, seed, and peel avocados. Fill peeled avocado half-shells with clam mixture. Top with buttered crumbs, if desired. Makes 6 servings.

## *Crab*

### ALASKA CRAB CROUSTADES

The avocado and crab duo is delightful served in this way.

3 tablespoons butter
3 tablespoons flour
1 teaspoon salt
2 cups milk
1 7½-ounce can crab meat,
  flaked

1 large avocado
4 toast cups (given below)
Paprika
Minced parsley

Melt butter, stir in flour and salt. Blend in milk, stir and cook until thickened; add flaked crab meat. Cut avocado into cubes and carefully stir into crab mixture. Fill toast cups with hot mixture; sprinkle with paprika and minced parsley.

*Toast cups:* Remove crusts from bread; spread butter on both sides. Press lightly into muffin cups. Bake in a 375° oven for about 10 minutes or until lightly browned. Makes 4 servings.

## CRAB ACAPULCO

For an elegant luncheon entree there is none better than this one.

¼ cup butter
¼ cup flour
1⅔ cups milk
¾ teaspoon salt
1 teaspoon Worcestershire
   sauce
Dash cayenne pepper
2 tablespoons lemon or lime
   juice

3 tablespoons sherry
⅓ cup grated American
   cheese
2 cups or 2 7½-ounce cans
   crab meat, flaked
4 medium-sized avocados
Salt
Toasted sesame seeds or
   toasted coconut

Melt butter; blend in flour. Gradually add milk, cook and stir until sauce thickens. Blend in salt, Worcestershire sauce, cayenne, lemon or lime juice, sherry, and cheese. Add crab meat and cook until heated through. Halve, seed, and peel avocados; sprinkle with salt. Heap crab mixture into each avocado half; sprinkle top with either toasted sesame seeds or toasted coconut, as desired. Bake in a 300° oven for 15 minutes, just until warm, no longer.

Makes 8 servings.

## CRAB-AVOCADO LUNCHEON ENTREE

Only occasionally does one find a main dish that has such satisfying results.

1 tablespoon butter
2 medium-sized avocados
½ pound or 1 7½-ounce can
   crab meat
Salt and pepper

3 tablespoons lemon juice
1 10½-ounce can cream of
   mushroom soup
Buttered bread crumbs
   (optional)

Butter a 2-quart casserole. Slice avocados and arrange in casserole alternately with layer of crab meat. Top each layer with salt, pepper, lemon juice. Over the top, pour the undiluted soup. Sprinkle buttered bread crumbs on top if desired. Bake in a 350° oven for not longer than 15 minutes.

Makes 4 to 6 servings.

## CRAB-AVOCADO NOODLE BAKE

Take the ho-hum out of menu planning with this unusually good main dish.

*1 8-ounce package Krinkly*
*(or other) egg noodles*
*4 tablespoons butter*
*2 tablespoons flour*
*Salt, pepper, cayenne (to*
*taste)*

*1¼ cups milk*
*1 7½-ounce can crab meat,*
*flaked*
*3 medium-sized avocados*
*4 tablespoons grated*
*American cheese*

Cook noodles until tender; drain. Melt butter, blend in flour and seasonings; add milk, cook and stir until sauce thickens. Add flaked crab meat. Halve, seed, and peel avocados. Put noodles in shallow baking pan. Place avocado halves, rounded side down, on noodles. Heap thick, creamed crab mixture into each avocado shell. Sprinkle with grated cheese. Bake, covered, in a 350° oven for 15 minutes.

Makes 6 to 8 servings.

## CRAB HONOLULU

Crab, avocado, and cream of chicken soup provide an adventure in eating.

*½ cup thinly sliced celery*
*1 tablespoon butter or*
*margarine*
*½ 8-ounce can cream of*
*chicken soup*
*¼ teaspoon curry powder*

*1 7½-ounce can crab meat*
*1 tablespoon chopped*
*pimiento*
*3 medium-sized avocados*
*¼ cup grated American*
*cheese*

Cook celery slowly in butter or margarine until tender. Blend in undiluted chicken soup, curry powder, crab, pimiento and heat

through. Halve and seed avocados. Heap hot crab mixture into unpeeled half-shells; cover with grated cheese. Place in baking dish containing ¼-inch warm water. Bake at 300° for 15 minutes.
Makes 6 servings.

## *Fish*

### BACON-TUNA WITH AVOCADO

This is a taste treat that deserves special appreciation.

4 slices bacon
1 tablespoon diced onion
¾ cup thinly sliced celery
2 tablespoons flour
¼ teaspoon salt

¾ cup milk
1 7-ounce can white meat tuna
3 medium-sized avocados

Cut bacon into ¼-inch slices; fry until crisp; crumble. Drain off bacon drippings except 2 tablespoons fat. To fat add onion and celery; cook slowly until soft. Blend in flour and salt; add milk, cook and stir until mixture thickens. Add drained, flaked tuna and half of crumbled bacon. Halve and seed avocados. Arrange unpeeled shells in shallow baking dish containing ¼-inch warm water. Heap each shell with tuna mixture and sprinkle rest of crumbled bacon on top. Bake in a 300° oven for 15 minutes.
Makes 6 servings.

### DEVILED TUNA IN AVOCADO HALVES

Serve this as a family supper dish or party entree with equal success.

3 tablespoons chopped onion
2½ tablespoons butter
3 tablespoons flour
1 cup milk
½ teaspoon salt
½ teaspoon prepared mustard
Dash cayenne

1 tablespoon chopped pimiento
1 7-ounce can tuna
3 medium-sized avocados
Lemon juice
Salt

Cook onion in butter slowly until soft. Blend in flour, milk, and seasoning; cook until sauce thickens. Blend in pimiento and flaked tuna. Halve, seed, and peel avocados. Sprinkle halves with little lemon juice and salt. Fill halves with tuna mixture and place in shallow baking pan containing ¼-inch warm water. Bake in a 325° oven for 15 minutes.

Makes 6 servings.

## KAUAI FILLET OF SOLE

For a delightful Lenten entree, this should certainly please.

*4 fillets of sole or other fish*  *3 tablespoons butter or*
*Salt and pepper*     *margarine*
*2 tablespoons lemon juice*  *Flour*
*1 large avocado*     *¼ cup table cream*
           *¼ cup toasted coconut*

Season fillets with salt and pepper; sprinkle with 1 tablespoon lemon juice and let stand 10 minutes. Halve and seed avocado. Cut fruit into balls or, if desired, into cubes. Heat 1 tablespoon butter or margarine in skillet. Dip fillets in flour, then brown on one side. Add another tablespoon butter, turn fish and brown on second side. Add remaining butter, cream, and half of avocado balls or cubes; heat just a minute or two. Remove fillets to serving dish; top with remainder of avocado balls or cubes and pour cream over all. Sprinkle with rest of lemon juice and toasted coconut.

Makes 4 servings.

## HILLCREST TUNA SUPPER

Nearly everyone likes a tuna main dish, and this one should be no exception.

3 tablespoons butter or
　margarine
3 tablespoons flour
¼ teaspoon salt
1½ cups milk

1 7-ounce can white meat
　tuna
2 tablespoons minced parsley
1 medium-sized avocado
Toast

Melt butter or margarine; blend in flour and salt. Add milk, cook and stir until sauce thickens. Blend in flaked tuna and parsley; heat thoroughly. Slice avocado and arrange slices on hot toast; top with creamed tuna.

Makes 4 servings.

## SALMON WITH AVOCADO SAUCE

It's the sauce that gives a regal elegance to the salmon.

4 to 6 servings salmon steaks
3 tablespoons butter or
　margarine
3 tablespoons flour
¾ teaspoon salt
1½ cups milk

Dash Worcestershire sauce
Few drops Tabasco sauce
1 medium-sized avocado
2 tablespoons chopped
　pimiento
Paprika

Broil or fry salmon; keep hot in a 300° oven. Melt butter or margarine; stir in flour and salt, add milk, Worcestershire and Tabasco sauces. Cook and stir until sauce thickens. Cube avocado and add cubes and pimiento to sauce. Arrange salmon servings on hot serving platter and top with avocado-pimiento sauce. Sprinkle with paprika.

Makes 4 to 6 servings.

## SHERRIED TUNA HALF-SHELLS

If you are looking for the unusual in an entree, you have found
it here.

2 medium-sized avocados
1 10½-ounce can cream of
  mushroom soup
2 tablespoons diced pimiento

1 tablespoon grated Parmesan
  cheese
1 tablespoon sherry
1 7-ounce can white meat
  tuna

Halve, seed, and peel avocados. Place halves in shallow pan
containing ¼-inch warm water. Set pan in a 300° oven for 10
minutes. Heat soup with pimiento, cheese, and wine; stir in coarsely
flaked tuna and heat through. Place avocado halves on individual
serving plates and heap with hot tuna mixture.

Makes 4 servings.

## TUNA SCRAMBLE

This is a hearty end-of-the-month inexpensive entree.

2 to 3 medium-sized avocados
2 tablespoons chopped onion
1 tablespoon chopped green
  pepper
1 tablespoon butter or
  margarine

6 eggs
½ teaspoon salt
⅓ cup milk
1 7-ounce can white tuna

Halve, seed, and peel avocados. Place halves in shallow pan
containing ¼-inch warm water. Place in a 300° oven for 10
minutes. Meanwhile, cook onion and pepper in butter or margarine
until tender. Beat eggs slightly; add salt and milk and pour into
onion-pepper mixture. Cook slowly, stirring from bottom of pan.
When eggs are partially set, stir in flaked tuna. Heap tuna-egg
mixture into avocado halves and serve at once.

Makes 4 to 6 servings.

## TUNA-STUFFED AVOCADOS

Everyone likes to serve an entree with a gourmet flair, and here is one.

| | |
|---|---|
| ¼ cup butter or margarine | Dash pepper |
| ⅓ cup bread crumbs | ¼ teaspoon Worcestershire |
| 2 tablespoons chopped onion | sauce |
| 2 tablespoons flour | 2 7-ounce cans white meat |
| 1 cup table cream | tuna |
| ½ cup grated Swiss cheese | 3 medium-sized avocados |
| ½ teaspoon salt | Lemon juice |

Melt 2 tablespoons butter or margarine; add bread crumbs and set aside. Melt remaining butter, add onion and cook until tender. Blend in flour; gradually add cream, cooking and stirring until sauce is thickened. Add cheese, salt, pepper, Worcestershire sauce. Stir over low heat until cheese melts, then add drained tuna to sauce. Halve and seed avocados; brush with little lemon juice. Fill centers of halves with tuna mixture. Sprinkle with buttered bread crumbs. Place in shallow pan containing ¼-inch warm water and bake in a 350° oven for 15 minutes.

Makes 6 servings.

## WARWICK TUNA CRISPETTES

You will find unanimous agreement about the goodness of this main dish.

| | |
|---|---|
| 6 tablespoons butter or | ¼ cup finely chopped celery |
| margarine | 2 7-ounce cans tuna |
| ½ cup flour | Bread crumbs |
| 2 cups milk | 2 eggs, beaten |
| 1 teaspoon salt | Fat for frying |
| 1 large avocado, diced | |

Melt butter or margarine and blend in flour. Add milk and salt; cook and stir until sauce thickens. Set aside to cool. When cool, blend in avocado, celery, and flaked tuna and shape into balls. Roll balls in bread crumbs, dip in beaten eggs, and roll again in bread crumbs. Drop into hot deep fat (375°) and fry quickly to a golden brown. Drain on absorbent paper. Serve very hot.

Serves 6 to 8.

## *Lobster*

### LOBSTER CURRY

For an intriguing flavor note, try this elegant curry.

| | |
|---|---|
| *½ cup finely chopped onion* | *2 10½-ounce cans cream of* |
| *1 clove garlic, minced* | *mushroom soup* |
| *¼ cup butter or margarine* | *¾ cup dairy sour cream* |
| *1 to 2 teaspoons curry* | *2 7½-ounce cans lobster* |
| *powder* | *1 large avocado, cubed* |
| *¼ teaspoon ginger* | *Cooked rice* |

Sauté onion and garlic in butter or margarine until soft. Add curry and ginger; cook 1 minute longer. Stir in soup and heat until hot and smooth. Add sour cream, lobster, and cubed avocado. Heat through but do not boil. Serve on mounds of hot rice. Fresh or canned pineapple and toasted coconut chips may be used as side dishes.

Makes 8 servings.

*Oysters*

## SEYMOUR OYSTER SCALLOP

Who ever heard of avocados and oysters in combination? Try this entree for a surprise.

2 medium-sized avocados
Salt
2 tablespoons butter
2 tablespoons flour
1 cup milk
1 7½-ounce can small oysters
  or 1 cup fresh oysters,
  drained

¼ cup finely chopped celery
Dash paprika
2 tablespoons capers
  (optional)
Buttered bread crumbs

Halve and seed avocados; sprinkle halves with salt. Melt butter, blend in flour and ¼ teaspoon salt. Add milk gradually, cook and stir until sauce is thickened. Add drained oysters, celery, paprika; cook a few minutes. Remove from heat, add capers if used. Place avocado half-shells in shallow pan containing ¼-inch warm water. Fill with oyster mixture and top with buttered bread crumbs. Heat in a 325° oven for 15 minutes.

Makes 4 servings.

# Shrimp

## AVOCADO NEWBURG HALF-SHELLS

Shrimp and avocado are ideal when the right taste combination is desired.

2 tablespoons butter or
  margarine
2 tablespoons flour
1 cup table cream
1 teaspoon salt
1 teaspoon paprika

¼ teaspoon nutmeg
1 chicken bouillon cube
1 7½-ounce can shrimp (or
  other seafood)
3 medium-sized avocados
Herb crumbs

HERB CRUMBS:

2 tablespoons butter
½ teaspoon celery seed

¼ teaspoon marjoram
½ cup dry bread crumbs

Melt butter or margarine, blend in flour. Stir in cream; cook and stir until sauce is smooth and thick. Blend in salt, seasonings, and bouillon cube. Add seafood. Cut avocados in halves, remove seeds, and hollow out each half slightly. Cube the removed fruit and add to creamed mixture. Refill unpeeled avocado half-shells with seafood mixture and top with herb crumbs. Place in shallow baking pan; heat in a 300° oven for not longer than 10 minutes.

*Herb crumbs:* Melt butter, add celery seed and marjoram, and cook 1 or 2 minutes until butter absorbs herb flavors, add crumbs, then spoon crumbs over filled avocado half-shells.

Makes 6 servings.

## AVOCADO NEW ORLEANS

Cooking is an art and, to prove it, here's a sample.

2 tablespoons butter
1 pound fresh shrimp or
2 7½-ounce cans shrimp or
other seafood
1 10½-ounce can cream of
mushroom soup or 1 10-
ounce can fresh-frozen
cream of shrimp soup
2 tablespoons sherry
(optional)

Salt and pepper to taste
¼ cup table cream
½ cup grated American
cheese
2 large avocados, diced
Bread crumbs (optional)
4 tablespoons sliced
pimientos

Melt butter; add shrimp and soup. Simmer slowly for 10 to 15 minutes. Stir in wine if desired, salt and pepper, cream and cheese; simmer until cheese melts. Individual ramekins or a casserole may be used. In either case, alternate a layer of diced avocado with a layer of shrimp sauce. Sprinkle with bread crumbs and heat in a 325° oven for not longer than 15 minutes, just until the sauce appears bubbly. Garnish with pimiento strips just before serving. Makes 8 servings.

## AVOCADO SHRIMP BOATS

This is an entree for guests who expect the unusual in food at your house.

2 tablespoons butter
3 tablespoons flour
½ teaspoon salt
½ cup table cream
½ cup Chablis or other white
dinner wine
½ teaspoon Worcestershire
sauce
1 tablespoon lemon juice

½ cup grated American
cheese
Dash cayenne pepper
1½ cups fresh shrimp or 2
4½-ounce cans canned
shrimp
3 medium-sized avocados
3 cheese slices

Melt butter; blend in flour and salt. Stir in cream, cook and stir until sauce thickens. Slowly stir in wine, Worcestershire sauce, and lemon juice. Add grated cheese and cayenne and cook over low heat until cheese melts. Add shrimp and keep warm over hot water. Halve and seed avocados and place half-shells in shallow pan containing ¼-inch warm water. Put in oven at 300° for 10 minutes. Remove half-shells and heap with shrimp mixture. Cut cheese slices into triangles. Top each avocado half-shell with triangle of cheese for a sail, using toothpick as a mast. Serve at once.

Makes 6 servings.

## CURRIED SHRIMP LOUISIANNE

A well-seasoned curry sauce laden with shrimp makes a palatable main dish.

| | |
|---|---|
| 3 tablespoons butter or margarine | 2 beef bouillon cubes |
| 1 small garlic clove, minced | ½ cup hot water |
| 1 small onion, finely chopped | ½ cup milk |
| 3 tablespoons flour | 1 4½-ounce can small shrimp or 1 cup shrimp |
| ½ teaspoon salt | 3 medium-sized avocados |
| Pepper | Salt |
| 1 teaspoon curry powder | Lemon juice |

Melt butter or margarine; add garlic and onion; cook until transparent. Blend in flour, salt, pepper, and curry powder. Dissolve bouillon cubes in hot water. Add bouillon water and milk to flour mixture. Cook and stir until thickened. Add shrimp and simmer slowly while preparing avocados. Halve, seed, and peel avocados; sprinkle half-shells with a little salt and lemon juice. Place in shallow pan containing ¼-inch warm water; fill each shell with hot shrimp mixture. Heat in a 325° oven for 15 minutes.

Makes 6 servings.

## DE LISO SHRIMP BAKE

Exotic avocado served on rice mounds and crowned with shrimp-cheese sauce is superb.

*1½ tablespoons butter*
*1½ tablespoons flour*
*½ teaspoon salt*
*1½ cups milk*
*¾ cup grated American cheese*

*1 4½-ounce can shrimp or 1 cup cooked shrimp*
*2 cups hot cooked rice*
*1 large avocado*

Melt butter; blend in flour and salt. Add milk; cook and stir until mixture is thickened. Add cheese and cook over low heat until cheese melts. Stir in shrimp. Arrange rice in shallow baking dish. Slice avocado and arrange slices over rice; cover with hot shrimp-cheese sauce. Bake in a 300° oven for 15 minutes, just long enough to heat thoroughly.

Makes 4 to 6 servings.

## EASY SHRIMP CURRY

This piquant curry is designed for curry fans to enjoy and inexperienced cooks to prepare.

*¼ cup finely chopped onions*
*1 tablespoon butter or margarine*
*1 10½-ounce can cream of mushroom soup*

*¼ cup milk*
*½ teaspoon curry powder*
*1 4½-ounce can shrimp*
*1 medium-sized avocado*
*Hot cooked rice*

Cook onions very slowly in butter or margarine for 5 minutes. Add soup and gradually blend in milk. Stir in curry powder, shrimp, and heat thoroughly. Cube avocado and carefully stir cubes into hot mixture; heat a minute longer, just enough to warm the avocado cubes. Serve at once over hot rice.

Makes 4 servings.

## SAN CLEMENTE CURRY

Shrimp, avocado, and sour cream form the basis for this smooth curry.

2 4½-ounce cans shrimp or 1
    12-ounce package frozen
    shrimp
1 tablespoon butter or
    margarine
½ teaspoon curry powder
1¼ teaspoons salt
1 medium-sized tomato,
    chopped

1 medium-sized onion,
    chopped
2 tablespoons lemon juice
1 cup dairy sour cream
3 or 4 small avocados
Hot rice

If frozen shrimp, cook as package directs, shell and devein, or, if canned, drain liquid. Melt butter or margarine with curry powder and salt; add chopped tomato and onion; cook until soft. Add lemon juice, shrimp, sour cream; heat thoroughly but do not overcook. Halve, seed, and peel avocados. Fill peeled shells with hot curry sauce and serve over hot rice. Chutney may be served as a side dish if desired.

Makes 6 to 8 servings.

## SHRIMP-AVOCADO HALF-SHELLS

There should be compliments when this buffet offering makes its debut.

½ cup chopped onion
1½ cups thinly sliced celery
3 tablespoons butter or
    margarine
Dash Tabasco sauce
½ teaspoon chili powder
¼ teaspoon thyme
Pepper and salt

3 cups chopped tomatoes
3 tablespoons flour
2 4½-ounce cans shrimp or 2
    cups cooked shrimp
¼ cup minced parsley
4 medium-sized avocados
Lemon juice

Cook onion and celery in butter or margarine slowly for 5 minutes. Add Tabasco sauce, chili powder, thyme, pepper, ¾ teaspoon salt, and tomatoes. Cook slowly together for 15 to 20 minutes. Blend flour with enough cold water to make a paste. Stir paste into tomato mixture, cook and stir until thickens. Stir in shrimp and parsley and heat thoroughly. Halve and seed avocados; sprinkle with lemon juice and little salt. Spoon shrimp filling into half-shells and serve at once.

Makes 8 servings.

## SPICY SHRIMP-AVOCADO ENTREE

Use this eye-appealing and zesty main dish to perk up almost any meal.

| | |
|---|---|
| 2 tablespoons butter or margarine | Dash Worcestershire sauce |
| 1 tablespoon chopped onion | 1 tablespoon vinegar |
| 2 tablespoons flour | ¼ teaspoon sugar |
| ½ teaspoon chili powder | 1 4½-ounce can shrimp |
| ¾ cup tomato juice | 2 medium-sized avocados |
| ½ teaspoon prepared horseradish | |

Melt butter or margarine, add onion and cook slowly until soft. Blend in flour and chili powder. Add tomato juice; cook and stir until thickened. Blend in horseradish, Worcestershire sauce, vinegar, and sugar. Add shrimp and heat thoroughly. Halve and seed avocados. Place half-shells on serving dish and heap centers with piping-hot shrimp-tomato mixture. You may serve rice as a side dish.

Makes 4 servings.

# VEGETABLE ENTREES

## AVOCADO À LA KING

If you haven't tried an avocado-vegetable entree, here's your chance.

*2 pimientos, diced*
*1½ cups sautéed fresh mushrooms or 1 8-ounce can sliced mushrooms*

*1 cup standard white sauce*
*2 large avocados, cubed*

Add pimientos and mushrooms to white sauce. Just before serving, add cubed avocados to hot white sauce mixture. Serve in *croustades*, patty shells, or over toast, rice, spaghetti, macaroni, or noodles. Makes 4 to 6 servings.

## AVOCADO CELERY ROOT ENTREE

For an adventure in eating, prepare this very different vegetable-avocado combination.

*1 large avocado*
*Salt*
*1 cup diced cooked celery root*

*1½ cups standard white sauce*
*Pepper*
*2 tablespoons diced pimiento*
*Toast*

Cube avocado; sprinkle with salt. Combine celery root, white sauce, salt and pepper. Heat slowly to boiling point. Remove from heat; add cubed avocado and pimiento. Serve hot on toast. Makes 4 servings.

## AVOCADO ENCHILADAS

Here's an almost perfect entree for a cold day, a barbecue, or almost any occasion.

6 corn tortillas
1 4-ounce can green or red
 chili sauce
1 medium-sized avocado,
 sliced

1 small onion, finely chopped
1 cup (or more) grated
 Cheddar cheese

Dip each tortilla in dish containing half of chili sauce. Heat in greased skillet one at a time, until barely brown but still flexible. Into each tortilla put thin slices of avocado, small amount of onion and cheese; roll up like small jelly roll. Place all in greased shallow baking dish; pour remaining sauce over enchiladas. Sprinkle generously with cheese and bake in a 350° oven for 15 to 20 minutes. Serve very hot.

Makes 6 servings.

## AVOCADO ITALIA

This is a meatless main dish inspired by Italian kitchens.

1 large or 2 medium-sized
 eggplants
3 tablespoons cooking oil
2 teaspoons salt
1 cup diced tomatoes
¼ cup finely chopped onion

½ teaspoon orégano
¼ teaspoon garlic salt
2 medium-sized avocados
Lemon juice
3 slices mozzarella cheese
Paprika

Cut eggplants lengthwise into halves; scoop out about half of inside, leaving shell about ½-inch thick. Dice the part removed; sprinkle with salt. Bake eggplant half-shells in a 350° oven about 20 minutes or until tender. Meanwhile, heat oil in skillet; add diced eggplant and cook over low heat about 3 minutes. Add tomatoes, onion, orégano, remaining salt, and garlic salt. Cover and cook about 10 minutes. Halve, seed, and peel avocados. Cut 1 avocado into slices; sprinkle with lemon juice. Cube other avocado and

*Crab-Avocado Luncheon Entree.* An avocado and seafood entree is guaranteed to impress guests with the hostess's culinary skill. (page 154)

*Avocado Shrimp Rafts.* These sandwiches are distinctive in flavor, color, and nutrition. (page 179)

15

fold into eggplant-tomato mixture. Spoon mixture into eggplant shells. Top with cheese; broil until cheese melts. Just before serving, garnish with avocado slices and paprika.
Makes 4 to 6 servings.

## AVOCADO MUSHROOM TREAT

Make your next luncheon one to be remembered because of this treat.

2 or 3 medium-sized avocados
Salt
1 8-ounce can sliced
  mushrooms or 1 cup
  sautéed mushrooms
¾ 10½-ounce can cream of
  mushroom soup

2 tablespoons chopped
  pimiento
¼ teaspoon paprika
Potato chips, crushed, or
  buttered bread crumbs

Halve and seed avocados; sprinkle half-shells with few grains salt. Combine mushrooms, soup, pimiento, salt to taste, paprika and heat to boiling. Place half-shells in shallow baking pan containing ¼-inch warm water. Fill half-shells with mushroom mixture and heat in a 350° oven for 15 minutes. Remove from oven; sprinkle tops with crushed potato chips or buttered crumbs. Serve at once.
Makes 4 to 6 servings.

## CORN-STUFFED AVOCADO

This is a meatless entree that is both different and satisfying.

3 medium-sized avocados
Fresh lemon juice
1 small clove garlic, minced
¼ cup finely chopped onion
¼ cup cooking oil
2 tablespoons flour
1 teaspoon chili powder

½ teaspoon salt
¾ cup tomato juice
1 cup drained whole kernel
  corn
¾ cup grated American
  cheese
Crushed potato chips

Halve, peel, and seed avocados; sprinkle half-shells with lemon juice. Set half-shells in shallow baking dish containing ¼-inch warm water and heat in a 300° oven for 15 minutes. Meanwhile, sauté garlic and onion in oil over low heat until tender. Blend in flour, chili powder, and salt. Gradually add tomato juice; cook and stir until thickened. Stir in corn and cheese and continue cooking until corn is heated through and cheese is melted. Spoon into centers of warm avocado shells and top with crushed potato chips. Makes 6 servings.

## HALF-SHELL VEGETABLE SCALLOP

Serve a meatless main dish that is unusual and wholesome.

2 medium-sized avocados
Salt
1½ cups standard white
   sauce
⅓ cup chopped pimiento

1½ cups cooked or canned
   green asparagus, diced
8 thin strips bacon or ¼ cup
   grated American cheese

Halve and seed avocados; sprinkle half-shells with salt. Combine white sauce, pimiento, and asparagus, stirring as little as possible. Put half-shells into shallow baking dish containing ¼-inch warm water; fill centers with creamed mixture. Top each with 2 strips of bacon or grated cheese. Heat in a 350° oven for 10 minutes. Makes 4 servings.

## HOT STUFFED AVOCADOS

This is a flavorful, satisfying, and extremely nutritious entree.

⅓ cup finely chopped onion
1 cup thinly sliced celery
6 tablespoons butter or
   margarine
4 cups bread crumbs

1 teaspoon salt
¼ teaspoon sage
Pepper
3 to 5 tablespoons hot water
3 medium-sized avocados

CHEESE SAUCE:

2 tablespoons butter
2 tablespoons flour
¼ teaspoon salt

1 cup milk
⅔ cup grated American
   cheese

Cook onion and celery slowly in butter or margarine until tender. Pour over dry bread crumbs, tossing to blend. Mix in salt, sage, pepper and sprinkle with hot water, just enough to moisten slightly. Halve, seed, and peel avocados. Heap crumb stuffing into halves. Arrange in shallow baking dish containing ¼-inch warm water and heat in a 350° oven for only 10 minutes. Remove to serving platter and top with hot cheese sauce.

*Cheese Sauce:* Melt butter; blend in flour and salt. Add milk, cook and stir until mixture thickens. Add cheese and stir over low heat until cheese melts.

Makes 6 servings.

## MEXICAN STUFFED AVOCADO

Here is a meatless entree that is quite out of the ordinary.

*1 cup thinly sliced celery*
*2 tablespoons chopped green pepper*
*1 tablespoon butter or margarine*

*½ 10½-ounce can condensed cream of tomato soup*
*¼ teaspoon chili powder*
*1 cup grated American cheese*
*3 medium-sized avocados*

Cook celery and green pepper slowly in butter or margarine until tender. Stir in tomato soup and chili powder; heat to boiling. Remove from heat and stir in cheese. Halve and seed avocados. Place half-shells in shallow baking pan containing ¼-inch warm water. Fill shells with tomato-cheese mixture. Heat in a 300° oven for 15 minutes. Serve very hot.

Makes 6 servings.

## SOUVENIR LUNCHEON ENTREE

Corn, avocado, and tomato sauce make a colorful and tasty combination.

1 medium-sized avocado
1½ cups cream-style corn
½ cup tomato sauce
1 teaspoon chili powder

2 tablespoons flour
¼ teaspoon salt
Toast

Cube avocado. Combine corn, tomato sauce, chili powder, flour, and salt, blending well. Cook and stir until thickened. Remove from heat; stir in avocado cubes and serve over toast.
Makes 4 servings.

## TOMATO STUFFED WITH AVOCADO

Serve an unusual main dish that has fine flavor and color combined.

4 medium-sized tomatoes
Salt and pepper, to taste
2 medium-sized avocados,
    cubed

¼ cup shredded American
    cheese

Scoop out tomatoes; turn upside down on absorbent paper to drain. Season with salt and pepper. Fill each cavity with avocado cubes and top with shredded cheese. Bake in a 350° oven for 15 minutes until cheese is bubbly and slightly brown.
Makes 4 servings.

# "QUICKIE" IDEAS

## MEAT

*Avochili:* Fill avocado half-shells with chili or chili con carne. Place a triangle of American cheese on top. Run under broiler about 2 minutes to melt cheese. *Ole!*

## POULTRY

*Creamed chicken, California style:* Cover hot toast or rice with avocado slices; spoon over hot creamed chicken.

*Southern California chicken:* Dice avocado into hot cream chicken gravy and serve with fried chicken.

## SEAFOOD

*Main-dish-mate:* Dip avocado slices in lemon juice, then in bread crumbs seasoned with salt, pepper, and a little curry powder. Broil just 2 minutes until crumbs are lightly browned. Serve at once with fish or meat.

For that hot day luncheon, put a dollop of sour cream and a dab of caviar into an avocado half-shell.

## VEGETABLES

*Vegetable glamor:* Blend mashed avocado with softened cream cheese and mayonnaise or sour cream; season with salt and pepper. Serve as topping for baked potatoes, boiled cauliflower, spinach, or broccoli.

Give individuality to Lenten or meatless meals by adding avocado cubes to creamed sauces, such as creamed peas. Do not cook; add cubes just before serving.

For a change, try mashed avocado seasoned with French dressing on hot vegetables in place of butter. Try it on fresh corn, for example. Very good!

# Sandwiches, Bread, and Muffins

"A loaf of bread," the Walrus said,
"Is what we chiefly need."
—Lewis Carroll, *Through the Looking-Glass*

Nothing is quite so satisfying as the sandwich, which has become an American institution. The popularity of the sandwich is probably due to the fact that it can be prepared from so many varieties of breads and the choice of fillings and spreads seems endless.

No sandwich will ever be commonplace if one of the ingredients is the pale green, fine-flavored avocado. Whether the sandwich comes hot and bubbly from the oven, almost a meal-in-one entree, or is an attractive, flavorsome sandwich with avocado filling or decoration to be served on some special occasion, or is just an ordinary everyday sandwich, any homemaker can be assured that her use of avocado as an ingredient has provided a sandwich with both eye and appetite appeal. Sliced avocado, lemon- and salt-sprinkled, makes an excellent sandwich with little, if anything, added to it. Avocado slices added to sandwiches having cheese, cheese spreads, fish, meat, bacon, eggs, tomato, and lettuce—almost any sandwich filling—will result in an unusually good sandwich. This is made possible because the avocado flavor is so subtle that it combines well with almost any other ingredient. When many foods seem dull and uninteresting, a really good sandwich, especially one having avocado, will usually get a nod of approval.

# HOT SANDWICHES

### AMBASSADOR SANDWICHES

Serve a quick-to-make hot cheesewich and listen to the plaudits.

| | |
|---|---|
| 1 medium-sized avocado | 1 cup milk |
| Salt | Worcestershire sauce |
| 2 tablespoons butter or | 1 cup grated American |
| margarine | cheese |
| 2 tablespoons flour | Toast |
| ¼ teaspoon dry mustard | |

Halve, seed, and peel avocado, cut into slices; sprinkle with a little salt. Melt butter or margarine, add flour, ½ teaspoon salt, and mustard. Stir in milk, few drops Worcestershire sauce; cook and stir until mixture thickens. Add grated cheese and stir over low heat until cheese melts. Arrange avocado slices on toast. Pour cheese sauce over all.
Makes 4 servings.

### AVOCADO BURGERS

Here is a surprise hamburger that is a real crowd-pleaser.

| | |
|---|---|
| 2 medium-sized avocados | ½ teaspoon orégano |
| Lemon juice or salt | Crumbled blue cheese, grated |
| 6 slices bacon | Parmesan, or grated |
| 6 thin slices onion (optional) | American cheese |
| Salt | Tomatoes (optional) |
| 1½ pounds lean ground beef | French bread (optional) |

Slice avocados; sprinkle with a little lemon juice or salt. Cook bacon crisp; drain. Sauté onion lightly in bacon drippings until tender-crisp, turning once, then drain and sprinkle with salt. Mix beef with orégano and 1½ teaspoons salt; shape into 6 round patties about ¼-inch thick. Place onion ring on one half of each patty; top with 2 avocado slices, cheese, and crumbled bacon. Fold other half over the filling and pinch edges together. If desired, make 12 thin patties; put filling between them, pinching edges together all the way around. Broil or fry until browned on one side; turn and brown on other side. Garnish with remaining avocado slices. Serve with sliced tomatoes and hot buttered French bread if desired.

Makes 6 servings.

## AVOCADO LUNCHEON SANDWICHES

This is a hot, bubbly sandwich that will be enjoyed for its unusually good looks and taste.

6 slices rye bread             Salt
Butter                         Lemon juice
1 2¼-ounce can deviled ham     Thinly sliced American
Thinly sliced tomato               cheese
1 large avocado, sliced

Toast bread lightly and spread with butter. Spread half the slices with deviled ham. Cover remaining slices with sliced tomatoes. Arrange avocado slices over all pieces of toast; sprinkle lightly with salt and lemon juice. Top each piece of toast with cheese slice and place under broiler just long enough to melt cheese. Serve at once, open-faced, or put 1 slice on top of the other.

Makes 3 closed or 6 open-faced sandwiches.

## AVOCADO SHRIMP RAFTS

These little sandwiches have honest open faces!

2 medium-sized avocados
Lemon juice
6 slices bread (rye, whole
    wheat)
Butter
1 small clove garlic, minced
2 tablespoons salad oil

1 4½-ounce can small shrimp
    or ½ pound fresh shrimp
2 tablespoons vermouth or 1
    tablespoon each lemon juice
    and water
Salt and pepper to taste

Cut avocados into 6 lengthwise slices; sprinkle with lemon juice. Trim crusts from bread and spread each slice with butter, then cut each slice in half. Heat garlic in oil; add shrimp and heat for 2 or 3 minutes. Add vermouth or lemon juice and water and cook for a minute more. Place 2 avocado slices on each piece of bread. Drain shrimp and arrange over avocado; sprinkle with salt and pepper. Serve at once. If desired, garnish with little lemon twists. Allow 2 halved bread slices per serving.

Makes 6 servings.

## ELEGANT TURKEY SANDWICHES

Looking for leftover turkey ideas? Here's a hot meal-in-one turkey sandwich.

2 tablespoons butter or
    margarine
2 tablespoons flour
½ teaspoon salt
¼ teaspoon dry mustard
1 cup milk

1 cup grated American
    cheese
1 large avocado
5 slices crisp toast
Sliced turkey
Paprika

Melt butter or margarine, blend in flour, salt, and mustard. Add milk; cook and stir until mixture thickens. Add cheese and stir over low heat until cheese melts. Cut avocado fruit into lengthwise slices. Arrange hot toast in bottom of shallow pan; cover with a layer of avocado slices and turkey slices. Pour cheese sauce over all; sprinkle with little paprika. Place under broiler for 1 to 2 minutes, just until top is slightly brown and bubbly. Serve very hot. Makes 5 servings.

## FLORIDA SUPPER SANDWICHES

Use leftover ham and help that after-holiday budget.

1 medium-sized avocado
2 tablespoons milk
¼ pound grated American
   cheese

4 slices bread
Butter or margarine
4 slices ham

Cut avocado fruit into lengthwise slices. Heat milk and add cheese; continue heating until cheese melts. Toast bread; butter lightly and top each slice with slice of ham. Cover ham with avocado slices and pour cheese sauce over all.
Makes 4 servings.

## FROSTED CHICKEN-AVOCADO SANDWICHES

You will agree that this sandwich belongs to an extra-special class.

Butter or margarine
8 slices white sandwich
   bread
Chicken slices
2 3-ounce packages cream
   cheese

2 tablespoons milk or cream
2 medium-sized avocados
Salt
Tomato wedges
Pitted ripe olives
Parsley

Butter bread slices; put chicken slices between 2 slices of bread. Blend cream cheese and milk or cream and spread the mixture on top and sides of each chicken sandwich, like a frosting. Broil for 2 to 3 minutes, until cheese browns slightly. Cut avocados in half crosswise; remove seeds. Continue cutting across avocados to make avocado rings; remove skin from each ring. Top each frosted sandwich with avocado rings. Sprinkle with little salt. Garnish with small tomato wedges, pitted ripe olives, parsley.

Makes 4 servings.

## HOT CRAB DELIGHTS

English muffins and crab meat provide a distinctive sandwich.

*4 English muffins, halved*
*1 4½-ounce can crab meat*
*2 medium-sized avocados, sliced*
*1 10½-ounce can cream of mushroom soup*

*¼ cup milk*
*½ cup grated American cheese*
*Worcestershire sauce*
*4 slices crisp bacon, crumbled*

Toast English muffins lightly on both sides. Butter the 8 halved muffins and cover with crab meat and avocado slices. Top with sauce made of mushroom soup, milk, cheese, dash of Worcestershire sauce. Broil until sauce is bubbly. Sprinkle with crumbled bacon and serve piping hot.

Makes 8 servings.

## SOUFFLÉ SANDWICHES

This is a perfect sandwich for Sunday-night supper or home-on-Saturday lunch.

*1 teaspoon instant minced onion*
*2 teaspoons water*
*6 slices bread*
*1 medium-sized avocado, mashed*
*Salt*

*Lemon or lime juice*
*1 egg white*
*1 cup grated American cheese*
*3 tablespoons mayonnaise*
*Cayenne pepper*

Mix onion and water; let stand few minutes. Toast bread on 1 side only. Cover untoasted side with mashed avocado and

sprinkle with salt and little lemon or lime juice. Beat egg white stiff, fold in cheese, mayonnaise, and onion. Season with a little cayenne pepper. Spread egg-white mixture completely over avocado filling. Place on cookie sheet; broil very slowly until cheese melts and top becomes puffy. Small canapés may be prepared in the same way.
Makes 6 servings.

## WAVERLY SUPPER SANDWICHES

You'll hear requests for seconds when you serve this sandwich.

*4 slices bread*
*1 medium-sized avocado,*
  *sliced*

*4 slices processed American*
  *cheese*
*1 medium-sized tomato*
*4 slices bacon*

Toast bread on 1 side only under broiler. Arrange avocado slices over untoasted sides of bread. Cover each with cheese slice and top with thin slices of tomato. Cut bacon strips into halves and place 2 half-strips on top of each sandwich. Return to broiler with sandwiches about 5 inches from heat. Broil until bacon is browned and crisp. Serve at once.
Makes 4 open sandwiches.

# COLD SANDWICHES

## AVOCADO BACON SANDWICH SPREAD

Make an easy-do spread for open-faced tea sandwiches or canapés.

*1 medium-sized avocado*
*1 teaspoon finely minced*
  *onion*
*1 tablespoon lemon juice*

*½ teaspoon salt*
*Bread or toast*
*2 strips crisp bacon, crumbled*

Mash avocado; add onion, lemon juice, and salt. Spread on fancy shapes of bread or toast (no butter needed). Sprinkle crumbled bacon on top of each. Makes 12 small open sandwiches.


## AVOCADO DAGWOODS

This is a midnight snack four-decker sandwich that could win a popularity award!

| | |
|---|---|
| *Butter or margarine* | *4 tablespoons chopped* |
| *8 slices bread* | *pimiento* |
| *½ 7½-ounce can white meat* | *1 medium-sized avocado,* |
| *tuna, flaked* | *sliced* |
| *Mayonnaise* | *Salt* |
| *4 slices crisp bacon, crumbled* | *Lemon juice* |

Butter bread slices on one side. On top of 2 slices, put flaked tuna and spread with mayonnaise. Cover the slices with another slice of bread each. On this layer put crumbled bacon and pimiento. Cover with another buttered slice. On top of the third slice, put sliced avocados; sprinkle with a little salt and lemon juice. Top with another slice of bread. Cut each 4-decker sandwich into finger or triangular shapes. Hold together with toothpicks. Makes 8 finger or triangular sandwiches.


## AVOCADO JELLY ROLL SANDWICHES

Fruit salad is appropriate to serve with these dainty sandwiches.

| | |
|---|---|
| *Loaf of thin-sliced white* | *4 tablespoons mayonnaise* |
| *sandwich bread* | *4 strips crisp bacon, crumbled* |
| *1 3-ounce package cream* | *Salt and pepper to taste* |
| *cheese* | *Few drops Tabasco sauce* |
| *1 large avocado, mashed* | |

Remove crusts from bread slices; roll each slice with rolling pin lightly so as to flatten. Spread each slice with a mixture of combined ingredients. Roll up each slice as an individual little jelly roll; fasten with a toothpick to hold. Put on cookie sheet; cover with damp cloth until time to serve. Remove toothpicks before serving.

Makes 20 to 25 jelly roll sandwiches.


## AVOCADO SEVEN SEAS SANDWICHES

Sandwiches can be nutritious as well as delicious; try this one.

| | |
|---|---|
| 1 4½-ounce can small shrimp | 2 tablespoons mayonnaise |
| 1 8¾-ounce can pineapple | 4 dinner rolls or burger buns |
| tidbits | Parsley or watercress |
| 1 medium-sized avocado | (optional) |
| 1 tablespoon chili sauce | |

Drain shrimp. Drain pineapple, reserving 1 tablespoon syrup. Dice avocado and combine with shrimp and pineapple. Mix chili sauce and mayonnaise; carefully add to diced avocado, shrimp, and pineapple mixture. Cut thin slice off top of each roll or bun; scoop out part of the center. Fill centers with the mixture. Return tops to rolls and garnish with parsley or watercress if desired.

Makes 4 servings.


## AVOCADO SWISS SANDWICHES

Avocado is a perfect foil for the mild, gently-flavored cheese.

| | |
|---|---|
| 1 medium-sized avocado, sliced | 12 thin slices buttered white bread |
| Salt | Lettuce |
| Lemon or lime juice | 4 slices processed Swiss cheese |

Sprinkle avocado slices with a little salt and lemon or lime juice. Arrange a layer of sliced avocado on 4 slices of buttered bread. Top with second slice of buttered bread. Top with a lettuce leaf, then a slice of cheese. Top with a third slice of buttered bread.

Makes 4 3-decker sandwiches.

## AVOCADO TOPPERS

These avocado "topper" sandwiches and a salad make a delightful luncheon.

1 3-ounce package cream
cheese
2 tablespoons undrained
sweet pickle relish
4 or 5 slices hot buttered
toast

1 medium-sized avocado,
sliced
Lemon juice
Salt

Soften cream cheese and blend in sweet pickle relish. Spread on toast. Put avocado slices over cheese-pickle filling; sprinkle slices with little lemon juice and salt.

Makes 4 or 5 open sandwiches.

## AVOCADO TUNA-BURGERS

Tuna-burgers are a novelty and youngsters should like them.

¾ cups sliced or chopped ripe
olives
2 7-ounce cans white meat
tuna
1 cup bread crumbs
4 tablespoons mayonnaise
2 tablespoons finely chopped
onion

¼ teaspoon pepper
1 large avocado
1 tablespoon lemon juice
Dash salt
1 teaspoon horseradish
6 to 8 toasted hamburger
buns
Lettuce

Combine olives, flaked tuna, bread crumbs, mayonnaise, onion, and pepper. Make into round patties and brown in skillet, turning once. Mash or sieve avocado; add lemon juice, salt, and horseradish. Put tuna patty on bottom half of each bun. Spread avocado mixture on top of each tuna patty. Put lettuce on top of avocado filling and top with remaining half of bun.

Makes 6 to 8 tuna-burgers.

## AVOCADO TURKEY CLUB SANDWICHES

This is a gala 3-decker sandwich for that special occasion.

*18 slices white sandwich
  bread*
*Mayonnaise*
*6 large slices white meat
  turkey*
*6 thin slices tomato*

*Salt and pepper to taste*
*Lettuce*
*2 medium-sized avocados,
  sliced*
*Garlic salt*
*6 slices crisp bacon*

Toast bread, allowing 3 slices for each serving. Spread one side of each slice with enough mayonnaise to spread evenly. Top 6 slices with sliced turkey and tomato slices. Sprinkle with salt and pepper. Top with lettuce leaf, then second slice of bread. Spread lightly with mayonnaise, then top with avocado slices. Sprinkle lightly with garlic salt, then top with slice of crisp bacon. Top with third slice of bread. Cut sandwiches into triangles. Spear each portion with a toothpick on which is stuck a cherry tomato or an olive.

Makes 6 sandwiches cut into triangles.


## BIG BOY SANDWICHES

These sandwiches are popular with young people.

*1 medium-sized avocado,
  sliced*
*Salt*
*Lemon or lime juice*
*¾ cup drained pickle relish*
*¼ cup mayonnaise*

*Few drops Tabasco sauce*
*Butter or margarine*
*18 slices white sandwich
  bread*
*6 thin slices American cheese*

Sprinkle avocado slices with a little salt and lemon or lime juice. Combine pickle relish, mayonnaise, and Tabasco sauce, blending well. Place layer of avocado slices on 6 buttered bread slices; top with second slice of buttered bread. Spread pickle relish-mayon-

naise mixture on top of second slice and add cheese slice. Top
with third slice of buttered bread.

Makes 6 triple-decker sandwiches.

## CAPTAIN'S SPECIAL SANDWICHES

It's amazing what a slice or two of avocado does to a sandwich!

*1 medium-sized avocado,
sliced
Salt
Lemon juice
1 7-ounce can white meat
tuna*

*1 medium-sized dill pickle,
minced
3 tablespoons mayonnaise
Buttered bread
Lettuce*

Sprinkle avocado slices with salt and lemon juice. Drain and
flake tuna; blend together with pickle, mayonnaise, and a few
drops lemon juice. Place avocado slices on crust-trimmed bread that
has been buttered. Spread with tuna mixture and top with crisp
lettuce leaf. Cover with second slices of buttered bread.

Makes 4 large sandwiches.

## CLUB SANDWICHES DE LUXE

These sandwiches are just right for that next company luncheon.

*8 slices white sandwich bread
Butter
8 slices Swiss cheese
Sliced turkey, about 12
ounces
Lettuce
8 slices crisp-cooked bacon*

*2 medium-sized avocados,
sliced
4 thin slices tomato
8 large ripe olives
Thousand Island dressing
(optional)*

Trim crusts from bread slices, allowing 2 slices for each serving.
Cut 1 slice in half diagonally. On individual serving plate, put
one buttered slice of bread in the center and a diagonal slice on
either side of it. Cover center slice and 2 diagonal slices of bread
with Swiss cheese. Arrange turkey slices, lettuce, crisp bacon, and

avocado slices, in this order, on top of the cheese. Garnish the open sandwiches with slice of tomato on top and olives at the sides. Pass Thousand Island dressing if desired.

Makes 4 sandwich plates.

## CORONADO SANDWICHES

Requests for the recipe will be in order when you serve these sandwiches.

1 small avocado
¼ cup chopped ripe olives
1 teaspoon lemon or lime
  juice
¼ teaspoon salt

2 tablespoons finely chopped
  celery
4 slices buttered whole-wheat
  bread

Mash avocado fruit and blend with ripe olives, lemon or lime juice, salt, and celery. Spread on buttered bread and cut each slice across diagonally twice, making 4 triangles. Garnish each triangular-shaped sandwich with slice of ripe or green-stuffed olive.

Makes 16 small open sandwiches.

## CRAB SALAD CLUB SANDWICHES

Be prepared for praise when you serve these crab sandwiches.

1 7½-ounce can crab meat or
  1 cup crab meat
¼ cup mayonnaise
1 teaspoon grated onion
Dash Tabasco sauce
Salt

½ cup finely chopped celery
2 tablespoons minced parsley
8 slices buttered bread
1 medium-sized avocado,
  sliced
Olives (optional)

Blend flaked crab meat, mayonnaise, onion, Tabasco sauce, salt, celery, and parsley. Spread on 4 buttered bread slices. Top with avocado slices; sprinkle with little salt. Top with second slice of bread. Sandwich may be cut into quarters or left whole. If desired, garnish with ripe olives on a toothpick.

Makes 4 whole or 16 small sandwiches.

## DANISH SANDWICH SPECIAL

Avocado slices and a piquant mixture make this an unusual filling.

| | |
|---|---|
| ½ cup ground bologna | 4 slices buttered bread |
| 3 tablespoons pickle relish, sweet or sour | 1 medium-sized avocado, sliced |
| 2 tablespoons mayonnaise | Salt |
| ½ teaspoon prepared mustard | Paprika |

Blend together the ground bologna, pickle relish, mayonnaise, and mustard. Spread mixture on buttered bread slices. Cover slices with avocado; sprinkle with little salt and paprika.

Makes 4 large open sandwiches.

## DEVILED AVOCADO SANDWICHES

The excellent flavor and color combination make these sandwiches popular.

| | |
|---|---|
| 1½ tablespoons grated onion | 8 slices lightly buttered toast |
| 1 2½-ounce can deviled ham | 1 large or 2 small avocados, sliced |
| 1 3-ounce package cream cheese | Olives (optional) |

Combine onion, deviled ham, cream cheese and spread on toast slices. Top sandwich filling with avocado slices and cover with remaining slices of toast. Cut into quarters or halves, if desired, and garnish with olives.

Makes 4 whole or 8 half sandwiches.

## DUTCH TREAT SANDWICHES

Here's a sandwich calculated to please the men in the family.

*Salt*
*1 medium-sized avocado,*
  *sliced*
*2 tablespoons chopped pickle*

*½ pound liver sausage*
*¼ cup mayonnaise*
*12 slices buttered bread*

Sprinkle salt on avocado slices. Blend together the pickle, liver sausage, and mayonnaise; spread on buttered slices of bread. Place avocado slices over sausage mixture and top with second slice of bread.
Makes 6 sandwiches.

## FAVORITE AVOCADO SANDWICH SPREAD

This is a simple sandwich filling that seems to be a favorite.

*1 medium-sized avocado*
*1 teaspoon grated onion*
*½ teaspoon salt*
*2 teaspoons lemon or lime*
  *juice*

*Dash Tabasco sauce*
*1 small tomato*
*2 strips crisp bacon, crumbled*
*Hot buttered toast*

Mash avocado and combine with onion, salt, lemon or lime juice, and Tabasco sauce. Peel and chop tomato; drain. Add to avocado mixture together with crumbled bacon. Spread on buttered toast.
Makes about 1 cup filling.

## GOLDEN GATE CLUB SANDWICH

Here is a San Francisco version of the ever-popular club sandwich.

1 medium-sized avocado
½ cup finely chopped cooked
   chicken
2 tablespoons mayonnaise
Salt
1 teaspoon lemon or lime
   juice

12 slices toast
Butter
½ pint or 1 cup small-curd
   cottage cheese
1 small tomato, sliced
Olives (optional)

Mash or sieve avocado and combine with chicken, mayonnaise, ¼ teaspoon salt, and lemon or lime juice. Remove crusts from toast and butter lightly. For each sandwich, spread avocado mixture on first slice. Top with second toast slice; spread with cottage cheese. Arrange thin tomato slice over cottage cheese; sprinkle with salt. Top with third slice of toast. Insert toothpicks to keep layers together. Each sandwich may be cut into quarters if desired, with 4 quarters per serving. Olives may be put on top of toothpicks for garnish.

Makes 4 servings.

## HAMBURGER DELIGHT TOPPER

Hamburgers will never taste the same without this tasty topping.

1 large or 2 small avocados,
   mashed
2 tablespoons tomato catsup
3 tablespoons mayonnaise

2 tablespoons grated onion
3 tablespoons lemon juice
¼ teaspoon chili powder or
   dash Tabasco sauce

Combine all ingredients and spread on cooked hamburgers. Makes about 1¼ cups spread.

## LAGUNA SANDWICH FILLING

Leftovers often make the best sandwich, so try this one.

1 large avocado
⅔ cup veal, beef, or other
   cooked meat, diced

1½ teaspoons salt
2 teaspoons lemon or lime
   juice

Mash avocado and combine with the remaining ingredients.
Makes about 1⅓ cups filling.

## NORWAY SANDWICH SPREAD

Here's an almost unheard-of sandwich filling—but good!

1 small can sardines, drained
1 medium-sized avocado
2 tablespoons lemon juice

Salt
2 teaspoons tomato catsup

Drain sardines and mash to a paste. Mash or sieve avocado and
combine with sardine paste and rest of the ingredients.
Makes about ¾ cup sandwich spread.

## PACIFIC PARADISE SANDWICHES

You'll find that this sandwich has wide appeal.

2 4½-ounce cans shrimp or ¾    *Pepper*
   *pound cooked fresh shrimp*    *12 slices toast*
*1 large avocado, sieved*    *Butter or margarine*
*1 tablespoon lemon juice*    *12 thin slices tomato*
*1 tablespoon grated onion*    *Dried basil if desired*
*Salt*    *Lemon wedges*

Put aside 6 whole shrimp for garnish. Cut remaining shrimp into small pieces and blend with sieved avocado, lemon juice, onion, ½ teaspoon salt, and pepper. Spread toast with butter or margarine. Spread shrimp filling on 6 toast slices. Place 2 tomato slices on each of 6 remaining toast slices. Sprinkle tomato with salt and a little basil. Close sandwiches. Garnish with reserved shrimp on top of each sandwich and small lemon wedges at side of each one.
Makes 6 sandwiches.


## RANCHO EGG SANDWICHES

Egg sandwiches such as these offer extra taste appeal.

*1 medium-sized avocado,*    *¾ teaspoon salt*
   *sliced*    *¼ teaspoon curry powder*
*Salt*    *Dash pepper*
*4 hard-cooked eggs*    *12 slices buttered bread*
*⅓ cup mayonnaise*

Sprinkle salt on avocado slices. Chop eggs; blend with mayonnaise and seasonings. Spread egg mixture on 6 slices of crust-trimmed buttered bread. Place avocado slices over egg mixture and top with remaining buttered slices of bread.
Makes 6 sandwiches.

## SAVORY AVOCADO SANDWICH FILLING

Try serving French bread sandwiches, tomato soup, and crisp celery for a quick, flavorful lunch.

1 medium-sized avocado
1 cup well-drained navy
  beans

2 tablespoons catsup
Dash Tabasco sauce
1 teaspoon onion salt

Dice avocado and combine with remaining ingredients. Spread between slices of whole-wheat bread or on French bread or French rolls.

Makes about 1¾ cups spread.

## SEAFOOD SANDWICHES

This open sandwich will delight your guests and family.

1 5-ounce can shrimp
¼ cup dairy sour cream
Salt
1 medium-sized avocado

Lemon or lime juice
4 slices buttered toast
½ pint or 1 cup small-curd
  cottage cheese

Rinse shrimp and mash with sour cream and ½ teaspoon salt. Slice avocado and sprinkle with lemon or lime juice. Spread shrimp mixture on toast. On top of shrimp mixture put a layer of cottage cheese and avocado slices. Sprinkle lightly with salt.

Makes 4 open sandwiches.

*Kauai Fillet of Sole.* From sun-drenched Hawaii comes the inspiration for this dish, a taste-appealing entree dressed with delicately flavored avocado balls. (page 157)

*Avocado Burgers.* A hamburger topping that is as different as it is delicious. (page 177)

*Egg-stuffed Avocado.* An elegant way to serve eggs for brunch or a holiday breakfast is in avocado half-shells.

*Dreamwood Ice Cream.* Avocado ice cream, so velvety smooth and refreshing, is ideal for the summer menu. (page 204)

## TEEN-AGE SPECIAL SANDWICHES

This sandwich is as easy as ABC to make and is a specialty of the younger set.

| | |
|---|---|
| 1 medium-sized avocado, sliced | 8 slices whole-wheat bread |
| Lemon or lime juice | Mayonnaise |
| Salt | Potato chips, crushed |
| | Lettuce |

Sprinkle avocado slices with lemon or lime juice and salt. Spread crust-trimmed bread with mayonnaise and sprinkle 4 slices with finely crushed potato chips. Cover with avocado slices. Add lettuce and top with second mayonnaise-spread slice of bread.
Makes 4 sandwiches.

# BREAD

## CALIFORNIA AVOCADO BREAD

Avocado bread is especially adaptable for buffets, luncheons, bridge club events, or for fancy sandwiches.

| | |
|---|---|
| ½ cup butter | 2 teaspoons baking powder |
| 1 cup sugar | ½ teaspoon salt |
| 2 eggs, well beaten | Dash of cloves |
| 1 cup mashed avocado mixed with lemon juice | Dash of cinnamon |
| 2 cups all-purpose flour | 1 cup chopped walnuts or pecans |

Cream butter and sugar together. Mix all remaining ingredients in order given. Bake in medium-sized loaf pan in a 350° oven for 15 minutes. Lower temperature to 325° and bake another 45 minutes. Put on rack to cool.
Makes 1 medium-sized loaf.

## MUFFINS

### AVOCADO MUFFINS

Avocado muffins will certainly pique the curiosity of their partakers.

| | |
|---|---|
| ¼ cup sugar | 2 cups all-purpose flour |
| 4 tablespoons melted butter | ½ teaspoon salt |
| 1 egg, beaten | 3 teaspoons baking powder |
| 1 small avocado, mashed | 1 cup plus 2 tablespoons milk |

Beat together the first 4 ingredients. Sift dry ingredients and add to the first mixture, alternating with milk. Blend well but do not overbeat. Put in greased muffin tins and bake at 400° for 20 minutes.

Makes 12 large or 16 small muffins.

### "QUICKIE" IDEAS

*Toasted Sandwiches:* Many of the favorite fillings; chicken, tuna, or shrimp, are enhanced when topped with several slices of avocado that have been sprinkled with a few drops of lemon juice and salt.

Put avocado slices and thin slices of tomato on sandwiches with beef, ham, smoked salmon, or cold cuts.

Use curried mayonnaise, lettuce, sliced tomato, strips of crisp bacon, and sliced avocado for a toasted club sandwich. Just right for Sunday night!

With a 5-ounce jar of boned chicken, make a party sandwich in minutes. Add a little minced celery, Worcestershire sauce, and mayonnaise to the chicken and spread on your favorite bread. Top with slices of avocado and you will find the combination unbeatable.

*Summer supper sandwich:* Spread rye bread with softened cream cheese seasoned with a few drops of Tabasco sauce, onion salt, and prepared mustard. Top with thin slices of turkey, slices of tomato and avocado. Serve open-faced with whole spiced peaches, ripe olives, *rosé* wine.

*Avocado delight:* Spread toast with a cheese spread. Cover with sliced avocado and 2 slices crisp-cooked bacon for each sandwich. Serve a lime gelatin salad as an accompaniment and you'll have delighted partakers.

# Desserts and Dessert Sauces

"The setting sun, and music at the close,
As the last taste of sweets, is sweetest last
Writ in remembrance, more than things long past."
—William Shakespeare, *King Richard II*

Appetites may be somewhat jaded by the time dessert arrives at table. The accomplished homemaker or hostess knows that she must display finesse in the selection and preparation of a dessert that will be both attractive and tempting. If it does not stir interest and comment when it appears, it might as well have been omitted from the menu.

In case you have forgotten—and sometimes the two desserts do get confused—an ice is made with water, a sherbet with milk. No one can complain about too many calories when a sieved avocado is used as a perfect base for an ice, sherbet, or other desserts. The calorie count per serving is very small and avocado adds the cool coloring and smooth texture that no other ingredient can. Another distinct advantage of frozen desserts is that they can be whipped together in minutes, put in the refrigerator until serving time on that day or in the freezing unit, to be used later when needed.

In this collection of recipes for desserts using avocados may be found those just right for holiday dinners and parties; others for simple family meals. Any one of the desserts will bring the meal to a satisfying, delightful climax.

# FROZEN DESSERTS

## AVOCADO CRANBERRY MOUSSE

This is a very special, elegant dessert appropriate to Valentine's Day.

| | |
|---|---|
| 1 cup fresh cranberries | Few grains salt |
| ½ cup water | 1 small avocado |
| ⅓ cup sugar | 1 cup whipping cream |
| 1 tablespoon lemon or lime juice | |

Rinse cranberries, add water, and boil about 5 minutes. Force through sieve. Heat cranberry purée; add sugar and stir until sugar dissolves. Cool and add lemon or lime juice and salt. Cube avocado. Whip cream and gently fold in cranberry purée and avocado cubes. Pour into refrigerator tray and place in freezing compartment. Freeze until firm but not hard.
Makes 5 to 6 servings.

## AVOCADO BOMBE

For a beautiful dessert certain to delight, serve this one.

| | |
|---|---|
| 2 medium-sized avocados, sieved | 1 cup whipping cream, whipped |
| 2 tablespoons lemon juice | 1 tablespoon orange rind |
| 2 3-ounce packages cream cheese | 1 tablespoon crystalized ginger (optional) |
| ½ cup powdered sugar | 1 pint orange or lemon sherbet |
| Few grains salt | |

Chill a 7-cup melon mold. Mash or sieve avocados and mix together with lemon juice, softened cream cheese, powdered sugar

and salt. Whip cream and stir in grated orange rind; fold into avocado mixture. Turn into the chilled mold and line sides with avocado mixture, using back of spoon to form a well in center. Put into freezing compartment until slightly set, about 1 hour. Stir the finely chopped ginger (optional) into sherbet and spoon into well of the mold, being careful not to leave any air spaces. Cover with plastic wrap and freeze until firm. About 30 minutes before serving, remove mold from freezer to refrigerator. Just before time to serve, dip bottom of mold quickly into lukewarm water; run knife around edge, and invert on pretty serving plate. Serve at the table with thin orange or lemon wafers if desired.
Makes 12 servings.

## AVOCADO CREAM FREEZE

Nothing is more refreshing than a frozen dessert on a summer's evening.

| | |
|---|---|
| 1 cup table cream | 2 teaspoons cold water |
| 1 cup milk | 2 eggs |
| 1/3 cup sugar | 1 large avocado |
| 1/4 teaspoon salt | 1 tablespoon lemon or lime |
| 1 teaspoon plain gelatin | juice |

Combine cream, milk, sugar, and salt; heat just to boiling point. Soften gelatin in cold water and dissolve in hot liquid. Beat eggs and stir into hot mixture. Chill. Mash or sieve avocado; blend it with lemon or lime juice and add to gelatin mixture. Pour into refrigerator tray; place in freezing compartment at lowest temperature and freeze. Stir 2 or 3 times during freezing process. Reset temperature control to normal until ready to serve.
Makes 6 servings.

## AVOCADO HONEY ICE CREAM

This is a dessert worthy of a four-star rating.

| | |
|---|---|
| ½ cup evaporated milk | 3 tablespoons sugar |
| Few grains salt | 1 large avocado, sieved |
| 1 teaspoon plain gelatin | 2 tablespoons lemon or lime |
| ½ cup fresh milk | juice |
| 2 egg whites | 1 teaspoon vanilla |
| ⅓ cup honey | |

Combine evaporated milk and salt; heat to just below boiling. Soften gelatin in fresh milk and dissolve in hot milk. Chill thoroughly. Beat egg whites until stiff but not dry. Beat in honey and sugar, a small portion at a time. Carefully blend sieved avocado, lemon or lime juice, and vanilla into egg white mixture. Pour into refrigerator tray; place in freezing compartment with control at lowest temperature. Freeze until barely firm, then reset control to normal.

Makes 8 to 10 servings (about 1½ quarts).

## AVOCADO ICE CREAM, POLYNESIA

A fruit-flavored dessert usually pleases, as this one will.

| | |
|---|---|
| 1 envelope plain gelatin | ⅓ cup lemon juice |
| ¼ cup water | ⅓ cup lime juice |
| ¾ cup sugar | 1 8¼-ounce can crushed |
| ½ teaspoon salt | pineapple |
| ½ teaspoon each lemon and | 2 large avocados |
| lime rind | 1 pint table cream |

Soften gelatin in cold water in saucepan. Heat over low heat until gelatin dissolves. Add sugar, salt, rinds, and juices. Heat and stir again until sugar dissolves. Remove from heat; stir in undrained pineapple. Mash or sieve avocados; stir into cooled pineapple mixture together with cream. Turn into 2 refrigerator trays;

cover with foil. Freeze until frozen around edges. Turn into mixing bowl and whip until soft. Return to trays and refreeze until of serving consistency. May be made in an ice-cream freezer if desired.

Make 8 to 10 servings (about 1½ quarts).


## AVOCADO MARLOW

Invite guests to try this velvety-smooth avocado dessert.

*16 large marshmallows or 1  
  4-ounce package miniature  
  marshmallows  
1 cup milk  
1 medium-sized avocado  
1 cup table cream*

*Few grains salt  
1 tablespoon lemon or lime  
  juice  
¼ teaspoon lemon or lime  
  rind*

Cut marshmallows into small pieces or use miniature marshmallows. Add milk and heat slowly in top of double boiler, stirring until marshmallows are melted. Cool. Mash or sieve avocado and blend into marshmallow mixture. Add cream, salt, lemon or lime juice, and rind. Turn into refrigerator tray; put in freezer with control set at lowest temperature. Freeze until firm, stirring once or twice with a fork, then reset temperature control to normal.

Makes 6 to 8 servings (about 1 quart).


## AVOCADO ORANGE ICE

Here is a hot-day ice that is both distinctive and refreshing.

*2 cups fresh orange juice  
1 cup cold water  
¾ cup sugar*

*Few grains salt  
1 large avocado, sieved*

Mix orange juice, water, sugar, and salt together and stir until sugar and salt are dissolved. Add the sieved or mashed avocado. Turn into refrigerator tray; place in freezing compartment with control set at lowest temperature and freeze until firm. Turn into a chilled bowl and beat with rotary beater until smooth. Return to freezing compartment and freeze until firm. A nice variation is to use pineapple juice instead of orange juice and used only ½ cup sugar and you have an equally refreshing Avocado Pineapple Ice. Makes 6 to 8 servings (about 1 quart).

## AVOCADO RASPBERRY MAJESTIC

Avocados and berries are combined to make a successful dessert.

| | |
|---|---|
| 2 medium-sized avocados, sieved or mashed | Pinch salt |
| | 1½ cups table cream |
| 3 tablespoons lemon juice | ¼ teaspoon green coloring |
| 1 teaspoon lemon rind | 2 egg whites |
| 1 tablespoon orange juice | Frozen sweetened raspberries |

Mix together the sieved or mashed avocados, lemon juice, lemon rind, orange juice, salt, and cream. Add coloring. Chill in refrigerator until partially frozen. Fold in stiffly beaten egg whites. Pour into freezing trays with alternate layers of frozen raspberries. Cover with foil and put in freezing compartment for 24 hours. Allow to thaw half hour before slicing to serve.
Makes 8 servings.

## AVOCADO SHERBET IMPERIALE

No sherbet could be this smooth without the avocado.

| | |
|---|---|
| 1 medium-sized avocado | ½ teaspoon orange rind |
| 2 cups buttermilk | ½ teaspoon lemon rind |
| ½ cup orange juice | ¼ teaspoon salt |
| 2 tablespoons lemon juice | ¾ cup sugar |

Mash or sieve avocado and blend into it all the remaining ingredients, stirring until sugar is dissolved. Turn into refrigerator tray and place in freezing compartment with lowest temperature. Freeze until firm. Turn into chilled bowl and beat with rotary beater until smooth and fluffy. Return to freezing unit and freeze to desired consistency. Reset temperature control to normal.
Makes 8 servings (about 1 quart).

## CATHAY DELIGHT

This is a sherbet simple enough for a family meal but elegant enough for guest dinners.

| | |
|---|---|
| 1 medium-sized avocado | 1/4 teaspoon salt |
| 2 cups grapefruit juice | Crystallized ginger, finely |
| 1/2 cup sugar | chopped |

Mash or sieve avocado; stir in grapefruit juice, sugar, and salt. Pour into refrigerator tray and freeze until firm. Turn into chilled bowl and beat with a rotary beater until smooth and fluffy. Return to freezing compartment and freeze to desired consistency. To serve, garnish with bits of crystallized ginger sprinkled on top.

Makes 6 servings (about 1½ pints).

## DREAMWOOD ICE CREAM

Here is a dessert that will be the crowning climax of the dinner.

| | |
|---|---|
| 1 medium-sized avocado | 1/4 teaspoon salt |
| 1/2 cup orange juice | 1/2 cup sugar |
| 2 tablespoons lemon juice | 1 cup table cream |
| 1/4 teaspoon grated orange rind | 1 cup milk |

Mash or sieve avocado. Blend in all remaining ingredients. Pour into refrigerator tray; place in freezing compartment with control set at lowest temperature; freeze until firm. Turn into chilled bowl and beat with rotary beater until smooth and fluffy. Return to freezing compartment and freeze to desired consistency. Reset temperature control to normal. If desired, an ice cream freezer may be used to make this ice cream.

Serves 6 to 8 (about 1 quart).

## FAVORITE FROZEN PUDDING

Dessert fans will proffer compliments when they taste this dessert.

| | |
|---|---|
| 1 cup milk | 1 large avocado |
| ⅓ cup sugar | 1 tablespoon lemon or lime |
| ¼ teaspoon salt | juice |
| 1 egg, lightly beaten | ¾ cup whipping cream, |
| 1 teaspoon plain gelatin | whipped |
| 1 tablespoon cold water | |

Scald milk with sugar and salt. Stir into lightly beaten egg. Place over hot water; cook and stir until mixture coats spoon. Soften gelatin in cold water and dissolve in hot custard. Cool. Mash or sieve avocado. Add part of custard to avocado so that the mixture blends easily. Combine with remaining custard and juice. Fold in whipped cream. Turn into refrigerator tray and put in freezing compartment with control at lowest temperature. Freeze until barely firm. Stir thoroughly with a fork. Freeze to desired consistency and reset control to normal. Use ice-cream freezer for preparation if desired. Makes 8 servings (about 1 quart).

## FROZEN MELBA PUDDING

If you like a dessert that is brimful of tasty goodness, you'll like this one.

| | |
|---|---|
| 1 3-ounce package cream | 1 large avocado, sliced |
| cheese | ¼ cup chopped dates |
| ¾ cup whipping cream | 1 cup canned sliced peaches |
| 2 tablespoons lemon juice | 12 maraschino cherries, |
| 1 tablespoon sugar | chopped |
| ⅔ cup shredded pineapple | |

Cream the softened cream cheese; add ¼ cup of unwhipped cream gradually. Stir until smooth and add lemon juice and sugar.

Whip remaining ½ cup whipping cream and fold into cheese mixture. Combine carefully with prepared fruits. Freeze in freezing compartment until of desired consistency. Makes 8 servings.

## MARMALADE MOUSSE

Discover the subtle avocado flavor in combination with marmalade.

| | |
|---|---|
| 1 cup whipping cream | 1 large avocado |
| 4 tablespoons lemon juice | 1 cup orange marmalade |

Whip cream very thick but not stiff. Add lemon juice to mashed or sieved avocado. Fold into whipped cream together with orange marmalade. Put into refrigerator tray and freeze without stirring until the desired consistency. Makes 6 servings.

## PRINCESS FROZEN DESSERT

Avocado gives this dessert an extraordinary smoothness and flavor.

| | |
|---|---|
| 1½ cups fresh milk | 1½ teaspoons vanilla |
| ½ cup sugar | 1½ teaspoons orange rind |
| ¼ cup light corn syrup | ½ cup ground or finely |
| ⅛ teaspoon salt | chopped unblanched |
| 2 eggs, beaten | almonds |
| 1 cup evaporated milk | 1 medium-sized avocado |

Combine fresh milk, sugar, syrup, and salt; heat to just below boiling point. Stir mixture into beaten eggs. Add evaporated milk, vanilla, orange rind, and almonds. Mash or sieve avocado and stir into milk mixture. Beat until well blended. Pour into refrigerator tray; place in freezing compartment with control set at lowest temperature. Stir once during freezing process. Continue freezing to desired consistency, then reset temperature control to normal. Makes 6 to 8 servings.

## RAMONA MOUSSE

Here's a palate pleaser, so expect to be asked for seconds.

*½ cup sugar*
*½ cup water*
*½ teaspoon vanilla*
*2 medium-sized avocados*
*1 tablespoon lemon or lime*
  *juice*

*2 egg whites*
*Dash salt*
*1 cup whipping cream*

Boil ¼ cup sugar with water for 3 minutes. Cool and add vanilla. Mash or sieve avocados (about 1½ cups). Stir in lemon or lime juice and syrup. Beat egg whites with salt until stiff and gradually beat in remaining ¼ cup sugar. With same beater whip cream until stiff. Fold in avocado mixture and egg whites. Turn into freezing tray and place in freezing compartment with control set at lowest temperature. Freeze until firm. Reset temperature to normal. Makes 8 to 10 servings (about 1½ quarts).

## SEA-FOAM MOUSSE

Choose this dessert when you want something spectacular.

*1 large avocado, sieved*
*3 tablespoons honey*
*¼ teaspoon salt*
*1 teaspoon lemon extract*

*2 egg whites, stiffly beaten*
*1 cup whipping cream,*
  *whipped*

Combine sieved avocado with honey, salt, and lemon extract; blend thoroughly. Add to stiffly beaten egg whites a small amount at a time; beat well after each addition. Fold into whipped cream, blending thoroughly but lightly. Place in refrigerator tray; put in freezing compartment until of desired consistency, about 2½ hours. Makes 4 to 6 servings.

## SUMMER MOUSSE BELVEDERE

Here's a dessert for family and friends who like only the very best!

| | |
|---|---|
| 1 medium-sized avocado | Few grains salt |
| ½ cup cooked gooseberries | ½ cup chopped maraschino |
| 1½ cups whipping cream | cherries |
| ¼ cup honey | |

Mash or sieve avocado. To prepare gooseberries, cook until soft in small quantity of water. Remove lid to evaporate excess water during last minutes of cooking. Purée in electric blender or sieve. Cool. Whip cream and carefully fold into it a combination of sieved avocado, sieved gooseberries, honey, salt, and maraschino cherries. Turn into refrigerator tray and place in freezing compartment with control at lowest temperature. Freeze without stirring until firm. Reset temperature back to normal.
Makes 6 to 8 servings.

## TROPICANA ICE CREAM

If you want an exceptional dessert with extra goodness, prepare this one.

| | |
|---|---|
| 1 medium-sized avocado | 1 teaspoon lemon or lime |
| 2 cups milk | juice |
| ⅔ cup sugar | 1 cup whipping cream, |
| ¼ teaspoon salt | whipped |
| 2 eggs, beaten | ½ cup diced canned |
| ¼ cup syrup from pineapple | pineapple |

Mash or sieve avocado. Combine milk, sugar, salt and heat. Pour over beaten eggs, stirring briskly. Place over boiling water, cook and stir until mixture thickens slightly. Remove from heat and cool. Blend together sieved avocado, pineapple syrup, lemon or lime juice and add to cooled custard mixture. Turn into refrigerator tray; place in freezing compartment and set control at lowest temperature. Freeze until barely firm. Turn into chilled bowl and beat with rotary beater until smooth and fluffy. Fold in whipped cream and pineapple. Return to freezer and freeze until of desired consistency.

Makes 8 to 10 servings (about 1¾ quarts).

## UNFROZEN DESSERTS

### AVOCADO CREAM JUBILEE

Surprise your family or friends with this glamorous dessert.

| | |
|---|---|
| 1 3-ounce package lemon gelatin | 2 tablespoons sugar |
| 1 cup boiling water | ¼ cup dairy sour cream |
| ½ cup cold water | 1 medium-sized avocado, sieved |
| ¼ teaspoon salt | Fresh blueberries, strawberries, or raspberries |
| 1 teaspoon lemon juice | |

Add gelatin to boiling water, stir to dissolve thoroughly. Stir in cold water, salt, lemon juice, and sugar. Let cool slightly, then blend in sour cream. Add sieved avocado and blend until smooth. Pour into 6 individual molds or into a pan 8 by 8 by 2 inches and chill until firm. Top with sweetened berries.

Makes 6 to 8 servings.

### AVOCADO LIME MOUSSE

Here is an avocado dessert with a guaranteed success story.

| | |
|---|---|
| 1 3-ounce package lime gelatin | 1 medium-sized avocado, sieved |
| ½ cup boiling water | 1 tablespoon lemon or lime juice |
| 1 8¼-ounce can crushed pineapple | ¾ cup whipping cream, whipped |
| Pinch salt | |
| ½ cup mayonnaise | |

Dissolve gelatin in boiling water. Add crushed pineapple and salt; mix well and set aside until it begins to thicken. When it is partially set, add mayonnaise, sieved avocado, and lemon or lime juice. Carefully fold in whipped cream. Chill until firm enough to serve. Makes 6 to 8 servings.

## STRAWBERRY GALA DESSERT

All should agree that this dessert has genuine distinction.

1 tablespoon plain gelatin
¼ cup cold water
¾ cup boiling water
½ cup currant jelly
¼ cup sugar
½ cup fresh orange juice

3 tablespoons lemon juice
2 medium-sized avocados
1 pint (2 cups) fresh
    strawberries, washed and
    hulled

Soften gelatin in cold water and dissolve in boiling water. Add jelly and sugar; stir until dissolved. Add fruit juices. Chill until partially set. Halve, seed, and peel avocados. Placed peeled half-shells in deep dessert dishes. Fill half-shells with strawberries and cover completely with gelatin glaze. Pour any excess gelatin mixture around each avocado half. Chill for several hours before serving. Makes 4 servings.

## DESSERT SAUCES

### SUNDAE FRUIT SAUCE

This refreshing fruit combination may be used as a dessert sauce or as a fruit cup.

1 10-ounce package frozen
    strawberries
1 cup dates
2 bananas
1 orange

1 medium-sized avocado
1 cup drained fresh, canned,
    or frozen pineapple
Vanilla ice cream

Partially thaw strawberries. Pit and chop dates. Peel and slice bananas; peel and segment orange. Cube avocado. Combine all fruits and serve over vanilla ice cream or spoon into sherbet dishes and serve as a dessert fruit cup with crisp almond cookies if desired.
Makes 4 to 6 servings.

## SUNDAE SAUCE FOR CAKE

This sauce is so unusual that everyone will wonder what it has in it.

2 medium-sized avocados
⅓ cup lemon juice
1 8-ounce package cream cheese
⅔ cup chopped walnuts or pecans

6 tablespoons Madeira or sherry or orange juice
Sliced poundcake

Mash or sieve avocados. Blend in lemon juice, softened cream cheese, chopped nuts, wine or orange juice. Cover tightly with transparent or wax paper. Chill thoroughly. Ladle over sliced poundcake at the table.
Makes 8 servings.

## "QUICKIE" IDEA

When you have had a non-avocado dinner, try an impressive "Avocado Split." Halve, seed, and peel avocados and into each half-shell put a scoop of lemon or lime ice, sweetened berries of choice, and, if desired, a generous dash of rum. Top all with a little whirl of whipped cream.

# Cakes and Pies

"I will make an end of my dinner; there's
pippins and cheese to come."
—William Shakespeare, *Merry Wives of Windsor*

## CAKES

Be creative and bake an avocado cake. Discover how easy such
cakes are to prepare; how moist and flavorable they are. No icing
is necessary and many prefer cakes just this way.

### AVOCADO CAKE, SOUTH SEAS

Make this avocado cake—and listen to the plaudits.

2 cups sugar
¾ cup shortening
3 eggs
2 medium-sized avocados,
mashed (1½ cups pulp)
2⅔ cups cake flour
¾ teaspoon each allspice,
cinnamon, salt

1½ teaspoons soda
¾ cup buttermilk
¾ cup white seedless raisins
½ cup chopped dates
¾ cup chopped nuts
Sugar and cinnamon
(optional)

Cream sugar and shortening until creamy; add eggs, beating
well after each addition. Add mashed avocado and mix thoroughly.
Sift flour, spices, and salt. Dissolve soda in buttermilk; add alternately with dry ingredients into the creamed mixture. Mix well;
stir in fruits and nuts. Put cake batter into either 2 9-inch loaf
pans or 1 square pan 8 by 8 by 2 inches. Bake at 300° for 45
minutes to 1 hour or until done in the center. If desired, after

baking sprinkle top of cake with mixture of ¼ cup sugar and 2 teaspoons cinnamon.

Makes 2 9-inch loaf cakes or 1 square cake.

## AVOCADO CAKE IMPERIAL

Every hostess likes to impress with a special culinary creation, and here is one.

2 cups sugar
3 cups cake flour
3 teaspoons soda
3 tablespoons lemon juice
2 large avocados, mashed
 (about 2 cups pulp)

2 cups each chopped nuts,
 chopped seedless white
 raisins
2 teaspoons vanilla

Mix and sift dry ingredients twice. Add lemon juice to mashed avocado. Combine dry ingredients with avocado-lemon mixture, then remaining ingredients; mix together well. Fill greased and floured loaf pans half full of cake batter. Bake at 350° for 1 to 1¼ hours or until done in center.

Makes 2 medium-sized or 3 small loaf cakes.

## AVOCADO DREAM CAKE

This is the kind of fruity, spicy cake that keeps moist for a long time.

1½ cups sugar
½ cup shortening or only
 ¼ cup if avocado is very ripe
2 eggs
1 medium-sized avocado,
 mashed
1½ cups cake flour

½ teaspoon each allspice,
 nutmeg, salt
1 teaspoon soda
½ cup buttermilk
½ cup each chopped nuts,
 chopped dates

Cream sugar and shortening together until creamy; add eggs one at a time and beat well after each addition. Add mashed avocado and mix well. Sift dry ingredients. Dissolve soda in buttermilk; add alternately with dry ingredients, mixing thoroughly. Add nuts and dates. Pour batter into either 2 small loaf pans or 1 square pan 8 by 8 by 2 inches. Bake in 300° oven for 45 minutes to 1 hour or until done.

Makes 2 small loaf cakes or 1 square cake.

## PIES

The use of avocado as an ingredient in pies is so new that, if you want such a pie, you'll have to bake it in your own kitchen. The idea of using avocados for this purpose may sound strange but the proof will come in the baking and eating.

### ALOHA AVOCADO PIE

This pie will afford a happy aloha ending to any dinner.

| | |
|---|---|
| 1 15¼-ounce can pineapple tidbits | ¼ teaspoon salt |
| 3 eggs, separated | 1 medium-sized avocado |
| ¼ cup water | 1 teaspoon lemon juice |
| 1 envelope plain gelatin | ¾ cup dairy sour cream |
| ⅓ cup sugar | 1 9-inch crumb pie shell |

Drain pineapple, saving syrup. Beat together egg yolks, syrup, and water. Mix gelatin, 2 tablespoons sugar, and salt. Combine with egg yolks and cook over low heat, stirring until gelatin is dissolved. Cool. Sieve or mash avocado and mix with lemon juice and sour cream. Chill, stirring once or twice, until mixture is partially set and mounds. Beat egg whites; gradually add remaining sugar. Fold gelatin mixture and pineapple into egg whites. Turn into crumb crust and chill at least 4 hours.

## AVOCADO CHIFFONADE PIE

Want to be a hostess in the limelight? Serve this pie and you will be.

1 envelope plain gelatin
2 tablespoons lemon juice
¾ cup hot water
⅓ cup sugar
¼ teaspoon salt
¼ teaspoon grated orange
  rind

½ cup fresh orange juice
1 medium-sized avocado,
  sieved
1 cup whipping cream,
  whipped
1 baked 9-inch pie shell

Soften gelatin in lemon juice; dissolve in hot water. Blend in sugar, salt, orange rind and juice. Cool to thickness of unbeaten egg whites and fold in sieved or mashed avocado and whipped cream. Pour into baked 9-inch pie shell and chill several hours. Makes 1 9-inch pie.

## AVOCADO LIME PIE

This unusual pie gives lively interest to party menus.

1 large avocado
1 can sweetened condensed
  milk (not evaporated milk)
1 teaspoon grated lemon
  rind

½ cup lemon juice
2 egg yolks
Few grains salt
1 sesame seed 9-inch pie
  shell

SESAME SEED PIE SHELL:

2 tablespoons sesame seeds
1 cup flour
½ teaspoon salt

⅓ cup shortening
3 to 4 tablespoons water

Sieve or mash avocado (should measure about 1 cup). Combine condensed milk, lemon rind and juice, lightly beaten egg yolks and salt. Stir until mixture thickens; fold in avocado. Turn into baked pastry shell and chill well before serving.

*Sesame Seed Pie Shell:* Place sesame seeds in 9-inch pie pan in a 325° oven until golden brown, about 8 to 10 minutes. Combine flour, salt, and sesame seeds. Cut in shortening until particles are size of small peas. Blend in water and form dough into ball. Roll out to fit a 9-inch pie pan. Place in oven; prick bottom of crust with fork. Bake at 450° from 8 to 10 minutes. Cool and pour filling into pie shell. Chill until serving time.

Makes 1 9-inch pie.

## BENDITA AVOCADO PIE

For a light dessert for the end of a meal, this pie will serve the purpose.

| | |
|---|---|
| *4 eggs, separated* | *1 envelope plain gelatin* |
| *1 cup sugar* | *½ cup cold water* |
| *¼ cup lemon juice* | *1 medium-sized avocado,* |
| *1 teaspoon lemon rind* | *diced* |
| *½ teaspoon salt* | *1 baked 9-inch pie shell* |

Beat egg yolks; add ½ cup sugar, lemon juice, rind, and salt and cook in double boiler until slightly thickened. Soften gelatin in cold water and add to yolk mixture; cook until gelatin is dissolved. Cool. Meanwhile, beat egg whites until stiff, adding the other ½ cup sugar gradually. When egg yolk mixture begins to set, carefully fold into egg whites. Lastly, fold in diced avocado. Pour into baked 9-inch pie shell and chill until serving time. If desired, at serving time garnish with a small dollop of whipped cream and a slice of avocado.

Makes 1 9-inch-pie.

# Breakfasts and Brunches

"Life, within doors, has few pleasanter prospects than a neatly arranged and well-provisioned breakfast table."
—Nathaniel Hawthorne, *The Scarlet Letter*

Rather than a hurried weekday breakfast and with today's increasing emphasis on use of leisure time, the homemaker is discovering the possibilities of a late morning breakfast or a leisurely eaten midmorning Sunday brunch. A brunch for guests, for instance, need not be as fancy as a special luncheon or as elaborate as a dinner. It combines breakfast and lunch, thus allowing for a two-meal day. If prepared with a degree of originality and satisfaction, a pleasant mood can be created that lasts the day. A late breakfast or midmorning brunch need not be for guests; it can well be a special treat for family members on a lazy weekend morning or during vacation time. Whatever the occasion, the preparation need not be a time-consuming process. Breakfasts or brunches may include seasonal fruits, perhaps some kind of hot bread in addition to the avocado entrees suggested here. In providing attractive and exceptional fare for breakfasts and brunches, the homemaker will give proof of her capability as a culinary artist.

## AVOCADO BRUNCH SPECIAL

Guests will agree that this brunch special is the very best.

OMELET:

| | |
|---|---|
| 6 eggs | ⅓ cup milk |
| ¾ teaspoon salt | 1 tablespoon butter |
| ⅛ teaspoon pepper | |

SAUCE:

| | |
|---|---|
| ⅓ cup milk | 1 4½-ounce can shrimp or 1 |
| 1 cup diced American cheese | cup cooked shrimp |
| ¼ teaspoon prepared mustard | 1 medium-sized avocado, |
| Dash Worcestershire sauce | diced |

*Omelet:* Separate eggs; beat whites with salt and pepper until stiff. With same beater, beat yolks well and stir in milk. Fold egg yolk mixture into egg whites. Melt butter in 10-inch frying pan. Turn omelet into pan and cook 2 or 3 minutes over low heat. Bake in a 350° oven for 20 minutes until top is set. Turn onto heated platter. Top with sauce and cut into wedges to serve.

*Sauce:* Combine milk, cheese, mustard, and Worcestershire sauce; cook over low heat until cheese melts and sauce is smooth. Add shrimp and heat. Carefully put diced avocado into sauce and heat about 1 minute before serving over the omelet.

Makes 6 servings.

## AVOCADO EGG BRUNCH

Bacon and eggs never tasted so good as when combined with avocado.

| | |
|---|---|
| 4 slices crisp-cooked bacon | Dash pepper |
| ¾ cup soft bread crumbs | ⅓ cup milk |
| 6 eggs | 1 medium-sized avocado, |
| 1 teaspoon salt | cubed |

Cut bacon into ¼-inch strips and fry until crisp. Remove bacon and drain off all but 1 tablespoon fat. Toast crumbs in bacon fat. When crumbs are crisp, combine with bacon strips. Beat eggs lightly; add salt, pepper, and milk. Turn into pan in which bacon was cooked and cook over low heat, stirring from bottom of pan as the eggs set. When almost set, add diced avocado, bacon, and crumbs; finish cooking. Do not overcook. Serve at once. Makes 6 servings.

## AVOCADO OMELET SURPRISE

You will want to serve this omelet every time you have a breakfast or brunch for guests.

| | |
|---|---|
| *1 small avocado* | *Dash pepper* |
| *¾ cup small-curd cottage* | *¼ cup milk* |
| *cheese* | *3 tablespoons chopped green* |
| *4 eggs, separated* | *peppers* |
| *½ teaspoon salt* | *1 tablespoon cooking oil* |

Mash or sieve avocado pulp and blend with cottage cheese. Beat egg yolks until thick; add avocado mixture, salt, pepper, milk, and green pepper. Fold in stiffly beaten egg whites. Heat oil in skillet; pour egg mixture in and cook slowly until eggs are firm on top and slightly brown underneath. Place in a 350° oven for about 10 minutes, or until lightly browned on top. Fold over, slip onto hot platter and serve immediately. Makes 4 servings.

## AVOCADO PANCAKE PIE

Who ever heard of a pancake pie? Well, here's how you make it!

4 eggs, separated
¼ cup flour
1 medium-sized avocado, sieved
½ cup small-curd cottage cheese

¼ teaspoon salt
¼ teaspoon baking powder
6 link sausages, cooked
Catsup (optional)
Parsley (optional)

Beat egg whites stiff but not dry. Beat egg yolks in another bowl; slowly add flour, sieved avocado, and cottage cheese. Blend well and slowly add salt and baking powder. Fold egg yolk mixture into egg whites. Pour into an ungreased pan 8 by 10 inches. Press sausages lightly into batter. Bake at 375° for 25 to 30 minutes. Cut in squares to serve. A dollop of catsup and a sprig of parsley may be used as garnish.

Makes 6 servings.

## BAKED FONDUE

No fondue was ever so tasty and tempting as this one.

8 slices bread
¼ pound grated Cheddar cheese
3 cups hot milk
1 tablespoon butter
½ teaspoon salt
Dash pepper

4 eggs, slightly beaten
1 10½-ounce can condensed tomato soup
2 tablespoons chili sauce
3 tablespoons water
1 teaspoon prepared mustard
2 medium-sized avocados

Cut bread into 1-inch squares; layer alternately with cheese in 8-inch square baking dish, ending with a layer of cheese on top. Combine milk, butter, salt and pepper; stir gradually into eggs. Pour over cheese and bread; press bread into liquid to cover.

Place baking dish in pan of hot water and bake at 350° for 35 to 40 minutes, or until custard is firm in center. Meanwhile, combine soup, chili sauce, water, and mustard and heat thoroughly. Dice avocados and carefully add to tomato sauce. Serve at once with the fondue. Makes about 1¾ cups sauce.

Makes 6 servings.


## GOLDEN WEST OMELET

What a difference in taste when avocado is added to an omelet!

OMELET:

1½ tablespoons butter
8 eggs
1 tablespoon water

1 teaspoon salt
Dash pepper

SAUCE:

1 small clove garlic, minced
2 tablespoons cooking oil
¼ cup chopped ripe olives
3 tablespoons table cream

2 small tomatoes, peeled and
  chopped
1 medium-sized avocado,
  diced

*Omelet:* Melt butter in 10-inch skillet. Beat eggs with water, salt and pepper until blended. Shake skillet while eggs are cooking to keep omelet sliding freely. Continue cooking over slow heat until the soft upper layer is an even consistency.

*Sauce:* Heat garlic in oil for few minutes; remove garlic and add olives and cream. Add tomatoes and diced avocado to mixture. Heat over low heat until warmed through, no longer. Carefully stir in part of sauce into the egg mixture, reserving other half for top when omelet is served.

Makes 6 servings.

## EGG-STUFFED AVOCADO

Serve this only if you want an exciting new brunch main dish.

⅓ cup diced celery
⅓ cup bread crumbs
½ teaspoon grated lemon
   rind
½ teaspoon salt
⅛ teaspoon pepper
⅛ teaspoon ginger

¼ cup milk
2 medium-sized avocados
2 hard-cooked eggs, coarsely
   chopped
¼ cup buttered bread
   crumbs

Combine celery, crumbs, lemon rind, seasonings, and milk. Halve and seed avocados; scoop out part of pulp to make nest for filling. Dice the removed pulp and combine with eggs; then add to mixture. Fill avocado half-shells; top with buttered crumbs. Bake in a 375° oven for about 15 minutes.

Makes 4 servings.

## HENNY PENNY AVOCADO PANCAKES

Looking for an unusual way to use eggs? Here's a good way!

PANCAKES:

1 egg
1 cup milk
½ cup pancake mix of choice
1 tablespoon butter
2 medium-sized avocados

Salt
6 deviled eggs (your own
   favorite recipe)
Parsley

SAUCE PIQUANTE:

3 tablespoons butter
2 tablespoons finely chopped
   onion
3 tablespoons flour
½ teaspoon dry mustard

1½ cups milk
Dash Worcestershire sauce
2 tablespoons lemon juice
1 teaspoon salt

*Pancakes:* Beat together until smooth the egg, milk, pancake mix and melted butter. Bake on lightly greased griddle, allowing 2 tablespoons batter per pancake. Slice avocados; sprinkle with salt. Place 2 or 3 slices on each pancake, roll, and place in shallow baking dish. Keep warm in a 250° oven. To serve, place 2 rolled pancakes on individual plates. Top with halves of 1 deviled egg. Spoon Sauce Piquante over all and garnish with parsley.

*Sauce Piquante:* Melt butter; add onion and sauté slightly. Stir in flour and mustard; add milk and cook and stir until sauce thickens. Blend in remaining ingredients. Makes about 1½ cups sauce.

Makes 6 servings.

## SCRAMBLED EGGS DE LUXE

You'll wonder why you haven't done this before after you've tried this combination.

*Salt*
*1 medium-sized avocado, cubed*
*8 eggs*
*½ cup dairy sour cream*
*1 teaspoon prepared mustard*

*¼ teaspoon pepper*
*¼ teaspoon Worcestershire sauce*
*1 tablespoon butter*
*Paprika*
*Minced parsley*

Sprinkle salt on cubed avocado. Beat eggs with sour cream, mustard, 1 teaspoon salt, pepper and Worcestershire sauce. Melt butter in skillet; add egg mixture and cook slowly, stirring occasionally. When almost set, add avocado cubes and fold in carefully. Garnish with paprika and minced parsley.

Makes 6 servings.

## SPANISH OMELET WITH AVOCADO

For a special Sunday morning brunch, serve this golden omelet with tomato sauce.

OMELET:

6 eggs

1 teaspoon salt

⅓ cup milk

1 tablespoon butter

SPANISH SAUCE:

¼ cup chopped onion

½ cup finely sliced celery

2 tablespoons butter or
    margarine

1½ tablespoons flour

½ teaspoon salt

¼ teaspoon chili powder

1½ cups canned tomatoes,
    strained

1 medium-sized avocado,
    cubed

*Omelet:* Separate eggs and beat whites with salt until stiff. With same beater, beat egg yolks well. Stir in milk and fold whites into yolks. Turn omelet mixture into buttered skillet. Cook over moderate heat for 2 or 3 minutes until bottom of omelet is set. Place in a 350° oven and bake 15 or 20 minutes longer, until top is slightly browned and springs back when touched lightly. Cut into wedges and top with Spanish Sauce.

*Spanish Sauce:* Cook onion and celery slowly in butter or margarine until transparent. Blend in flour, salt, and chili powder. Add canned tomatoes; cook and stir until sauce is thickened. Add cubed avocado to tomato mixture; heat 2 or 3 minutes, no longer.

Makes 6 servings.

## "QUICKIE" IDEAS

*Avocado rarebit:* Heat condensed Cheddar cheese soup without diluting; stir in prepared mustard and Tabasco sauce to taste. Spoon over hot toast and garnish generously with avocado slices.

Mash avocado and spread on unbuttered toast. Top with orange or lime marmalade. So fresh-tasting!

Creamed chipped beef on toast becomes extra special when cubes of avocado and a little sour cream are added just before serving time.

Surprise the family by serving the breakfast eggs on crisp toast that has been spread with mashed avocado. You'll have requests for a repeat!

*Corned beef hash delight:* Spread 2 cans corned beef hash in shallow baking dish; heat at 350° for 15 minutes. Make 6 rounded nests in hash with back of tablespoon and drop an egg in each one. Continue to heat until eggs are set. When ready to serve, garnish with avocado slices that have been sprinkled with a little salt and a few dollops of catsup, a few sprigs of parsley. Pretty and so very good!

# Beverages

"I am willing to taste any drink once."

—James Branch Cabell, *Jurgen*

The semitropical avocado, having such a smooth, velvety texture, provides an ingredient for beverages which is not only unique in flavor but one which has high quality nutrition. Avocados are recommended particularly in combination with milk or carbonated drinks for children or for those needing high digestibility and food value in their diets. These drinks offer something entirely new in liquid refreshment.

## FRUIT JERRY

Who ever heard of an avocado drink? Try this one and see how delicious it can be.

1 medium-sized avocado,
 sieved or mashed
Few grains salt
1 pint vanilla ice cream

1 cup milk
¼ pint carbonated water or
 carbonated drink

Blend avocado, salt, and ice cream with electric mixer or use rotary beater. Add milk, then carbonated water or carbonated drink. Serve at once.

Makes 4 to 5 servings.

## LEMON-AVOCADO SHAKE

Don't miss trying this rewarding, flavorsome beverage.

1 medium-sized avocado,
 diced
2 lemons, peeled and cut in
 very small pieces

1 pint pineapple sherbet
1 cup crushed ice
1 12-ounce bottle sparkling
 water or carbonated drink

Put avocado and lemons into electric blender or use rotary beater and blend together. Add sherbet, crushed ice, blending well. Add sparkling water or carbonated drink; blend for a few seconds only and serve in chilled glasses.

Makes 4 to 6 servings.

## PEACH COOLER

Summertime is ideal for serving this cooling avocado drink.

| | |
|---|---|
| 1 quart chilled milk | 1 12-ounce can fruit nectar, |
| 1 small avocado | peach or choice |
| ½ teaspoon salt | 2 to 4 tablespoons sugar |

Be sure milk is icy cold (may be partially frozen, if desired). Mash or sieve avocado; combine with remaining ingredients in electric blender or use rotary beater. Beat at high speed until smooth and thick.

Makes 6 to 8 servings.

## PINEAPPLE AVOCADO SHAKE

If you want to serve a different kind of drink, invite neighbors to try this out-of-the-ordinary one.

| | |
|---|---|
| 1 quart milk | ½ cup sugar |
| 1 medium-sized avocado | 1 tablespoon lemon or lime |
| 1 8¼-ounce can crushed | juice |
| pineapple | Few grains salt |

Pour milk into refrigerator tray and freeze until mushy. Mash or sieve avocado and combine with frozen milk and remainder of ingredients in an electric blender or use rotary beater. Blend until smooth and thick.

Makes 4 to 5 servings.

## SUMMERTIME LIME FLOAT

No drink could be more delightfully cool on a hot summer's day.

1 large avocado  
½ cup fresh lime juice  
¼ cup sugar  

Few grains salt  
1 quart icy cold milk  
1 pint pineapple sherbet  

Mash avocado and combine with lime juice, sugar, salt, milk, and half of sherbet in electric blender or in chilled bowl using a rotary beater. Beat at high speed until smooth and thick. Spoon remaining sherbet into glass before filling with beverage.

Makes 5 to 6 servings.

# Index